LESSONS IN THE LINES

Hidden Wisdom in Movie Quotes

Dimitri William Moore

@lessonsinthelines

This edition published by Highpoint Executive Publishing
For information, write to info@highpointpubs.com
First Edition
ISBN: 979-8-9989720-5-8

Library of Congress Cataloging-in-Publication Data
Moore, Dimitri William

Lessons in the Lines:
Hidden Wisdom in Movie Quotes

Summary: "Drawing from more than 130 iconic films and television shows, Dimitri William Moore invites readers into a deeply personal journey through the quiet moments, overlooked lines, and forgotten exchanges that linger long after the movie credits roll."
–Provided by publisher.

ISBN: 979-8-9989720-5-8 (paperback)
1. Performing Arts 2. Philosophy

Library of Congress Control Number: 2026905394
Manufactured in the United States of America

Cover illustration by Keturah Rose, based on a photo by Tao Huang
Developmental feedback by Amy McGregor
Book Design by Sarah Clarehart

Special thanks to Polina and the Ecstatic Dance London community for inspiring me to write this book on March 29, 2025.

Special thanks to "As"

Contents

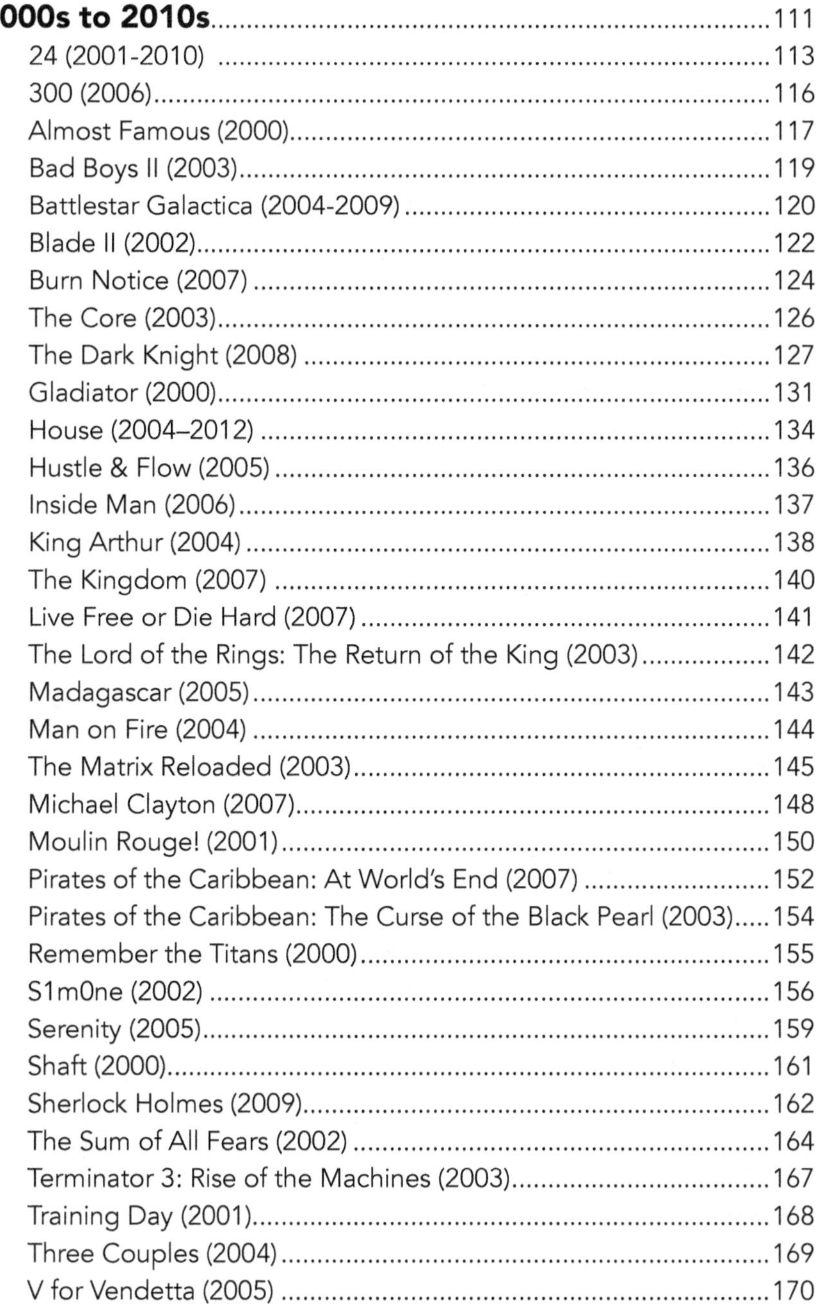

LESSONS IN THE LINES

Hidden Wisdom in Movie Quotes

Introduction

Movies are how I relate to the world. They're my love language, how I learn, how I teach, and how I make friends. They've taught me about history, emotions, and most of all, resilience. They've been my caregiver and my guide from the very beginning.

When I was young, I didn't understand the difference between movies and real life. I once thought that the gang violence of the 1980s couldn't have been that bad. After all, didn't all gangs roam the streets, singing and dancing with the occasional low-impact knife fight?

While I quickly realized that the carefully choreographed fight scenes in *West Side Story* were a work of fiction, I knew there were still lessons to be learned from the perilous situations our cinematic heroes face over the course of two or three hours.

Since then, I've spent my life drawing on various movie and television quotes in everyday situations. These are generally not the iconic super-quotes that have ingrained themselves into our culture ("I'm going to make him an offer he can't refuse"), but less-repeated statements that have nonetheless reached out and grabbed me. I might use them out loud to help others, or repeat them in my head to maintain my sanity and composure.

When I began writing these quotes down, I quickly realized that I've watched a *lot* of movies in my life! It reminded me that a friend once told me she'd "wasted a lot of time in her early years watching movies." I couldn't disagree more. I really believe that if you enjoy something, it's never a waste of time, and I set out to prove it by writing this book.

Ironically, the person who has given me the best quote of all doesn't come from a movie but from my own life. My mother, Jeannette R. Moore, once said to me "Do what you want to as long as you are happy and not hurting anyone." This quote has guided me through many triumphs and storms, so it's only right that I should dedicate this book to her.

1950s and 1960s

Batman: The Movie (1966)

Starring Adam West, Burt Ward, Cesar Romero,
Burgess Meredith, Lee Meriwether

The Quote

BRUCE WAYNE: *Where is she? Show me, Miss Kitka ... or I'll wreck this place with my dying breath!*

The Context

Bruce Wayne, a.k.a. Batman, and his date, Miss Kitka, have been kidnapped by his nemeses, Catwoman, The Penguin, The Riddler, and The Joker. Unbeknownst to Mr. Wayne, Catwoman and Miss Kitka are the same person, but he thinks she is being held captive in another location. Running out of patience, he threatens his archenemies with an ultimatum: "Show me Miss Kitka ... or I'll wreck this place with my dying breath!"

The Lesson

Seriousness can coexist with comedy.

The Batman TV series was always a fun watch. It was theatrical and over-the-top, much like the 1966 movie that followed suit. When Batman said this line, it stopped me in my tracks. It was a profoundly moving moment, in contrast to the rest of the film, which also included, among other things, a ridiculous exploding shark.

It showed me that if you suddenly switch up the vibe, you can throw people off guard. I have been in several situations where a little dramatic flair can be just what's needed. It can diffuse tension or increase it, depending on the moment's call for seriousness.

As a kid, I pictured Batman actually destroying the room with his final breath. It was a level of determination and resolve I would grow to emulate. Anyone who has watched the Batman films that followed will know he goes on to have a much more serious future. However, this moment sets the tone for how his character would develop in the years to come.

Cyrano de Bergerac (1950)

Starring José Ferrer, Mala Powers, William Prince

The Quote

CYRANO DE BERGERAC: *I have been robbed. There are no hundred here.*

The Context

This film adaptation of Edmond Rostand's famous play follows seventeenth-century swordsman and playwright Cyrano de Bergerac on a journey of love and bravery as he fights his enemy and helps another man win the woman they both love.

In this scene, de Bergerac fights a group of men alone, armed only with his sword, courage, and wit. Most people, when cornered and outnumbered, would look for a way out or cower in fear. But Cyrano steps forward, surveys the group, and proudly declares, "I have been robbed. There are no hundred here." Somebody told him there would be one hundred men. In other words, "Where is the challenge I've been promised? This is going to be an easy fight." He then takes on the group and defeats them all, saving himself and his temporary ward, Lignière.

The Lesson

I saw this movie when I was very young. While I didn't understand most of it at the time, I did recognize Cyrano's ego and bravado. This moment in cinema taught me courage: to stand up and face whatever force stands in my way. Though Cyrano has an inflated ego, he also has the skills to match the moment. Instead of running away or complaining about his situation, this quote most likely made the men he faced fear something.

Whether it's a big task like shooting an entire film, or a small task like doing laundry, I think of Cyrano's quote and adapt as needed: "I have been robbed. There is no three-hour film to shoot here." or "I have been robbed; there are not twelve loads of laundry to do here," and so on. Time will tell if that kind of inflated ego is warranted, but meeting a challenge with courage, humor, and wit will help you survive most odds.

Gunfight at the O.K. Corral (1957)

Starring Burt Lancaster, Kirk Douglas, Rhonda Fleming, Jo Van Fleet, John Ireland

The Quote

DOC HOLIDAY: *And Ringo? WAS RINGO THERE?*

The Context

Set in the infamous Wild West, legendary lawman Wyatt Earp is a man bound by honor and duty. Then there's Doc Holiday, the notorious outlaw who is dying of tuberculosis. Despite their differences, circumstances have brought them together to form a close friendship neither of them could have predicted.

When one of Wyatt's brothers is gunned down, Doc learns that his girl, Kate Fisher, was present at the meeting where the murder was planned.

Doc corners Kate and demands to know who was there. She lists several names, but one important name is missing: Doc's archnemesis, Johnny Ringo. It turns out that Kate has been sleeping with Johnny and refuses to betray him. Doc knows she's lying to him and asks her point-blank, "Was Ringo there?!" Did the man he hates have a hand in killing his best friend's brother?

The Lesson

If you must rage, rage responsibly.

What struck me most about this moment wasn't the line itself but how it was delivered. Doc has endured disrespect from everyone he has encountered, except Wyatt. He sees Wyatt as a brother, and by extension, Wyatt's brothers are also his own. They're the family he never had, so this moment feels like the ultimate betrayal. There's so much pain in his voice–stemming from his illness, his brother's loss, the loss of a loved one, and the revelation that someone he loved was involved with the enemy.

All of that erupts in a sudden, violent burst of rage, causing him to collapse.

Rage is always possible. Sometimes we know the answer before we ask the question. The answer can be hard enough to accept, but when someone doesn't say what we already know, that can make the moment truly unbearable.

The only lesson I can take from this is to practice acceptance. If you already know the answer, ask yourself if it's worth putting the other person on the spot. Will the question make things worse?

If you can't practice acceptance and rage is your only option, then at least rage responsibly.

The Guns of Navarone (1961)

Starring Gregory Peck, David Niven, Anthony Quinn, Stanley Baker, Anthony Quayle, Irene Papas, Gia Scala, James Darren

The Quote

MALLORY: *You think you've been getting away with it all this time, standing by. Well, son ... your bystanding days are over! You're in it now, up to your neck! They told me that you're a genius with explosives. Start proving it! You got me in the mood to use this thing, and by God, if you don't think of something, I'll use it on you!*

The Context

In this World War II action-adventure film, Captain Mallory and his team are on a daring Allied mission to destroy a Nazi weapons installation on an island in the Aegean Sea. One member of his team has a stellar reputation. Still, until now, he has only shown his ability as a naysayer, and Mallory has had enough of him questioning every decision and not pulling his weight. Holding a gun to his own teammate, he issues an ultimatum much like an angry dad to a lazy son. And it works!

The Lesson

Take a step to bring yourself closer to your goal, whatever that may be.

I have actually found myself in Mallory's shoes more often than not. People can promote themselves as being useful, but when the moment comes, they sit back and do nothing. Or worse, they impede other people's progress.

As a producer, in those moments, I encourage people to find a way to jump in and be a part of the solution. Or find the exit. There are situations where you have to wait until the right moment to take meaningful action, but that doesn't mean you have to sit by and do nothing. There's always something helpful you can do, even if that means preparing yourself mentally and conserving your energy, ready to strike when the time is right.

Spartacus (1960)

Starring Kirk Douglas, Laurence Olivier, Jean Simmons,
Charles Laughton, Peter Ustinov, John Gavin, Tony Curtis

The Quote

SPARTACUS: *Here's your victory. He'll come back.*
He'll come back, and he'll be millions!

The Context

Spartacus is a slave in ancient Italy who escapes and gathers an army of formerly enslaved people. They aim to leave Italy with their freedom. Standing in their way is the Roman General Crassus, a fierce protector of Rome's glory. His goal is to stop the slaves from escaping and to use that victory to gain total power. Between them is Antoninus, a former slave of Crassus who left to become Spartacus's top advisor.

After Crassus defeats Spartacus in battle, he forces Spartacus and Antoninus to fight to the death. The loser will be crucified at the entrance to Rome. Neither Spartacus nor Antoninus wants the other to face such a slow, cruel death. They reluctantly fight, with Spartacus emerging as the unfortunate victor. Upon Antoninus's death, Spartacus warns Crassus, "Here's your victory. He'll come back.

He'll come back, and he'll be millions!" Though Crassus won this battle, an uprising from Spartacus's many loyal followers is almost inevitable.

The Lesson

Empathy is the key.

Spartacus did not aim to conquer Rome or the world. He simply wanted to be free. He also encouraged others seeking freedom to join him in a common cause. Crassus could never understand that. He sees slaves as only slaves, and any attempt to escape is an insult to Rome "herself." Ironically, Spartacus understood Crassus and his motivation. He just lacked the numbers and resources to defeat him in the end. Although Spartacus was uneducated, he was empathetic. He understood both Crassus and the slaves, and he knew that the man dying in his arms would eventually lead to millions of people crying out for the same freedom.

Empathy can prevent conflicts before they start. The world needs more empathy. Without it, we will keep repeating the same pointless conflicts that have troubled human history since the beginning.

I have spent my life striving to be empathetic by examining and understanding the perspectives of others. Everyone has a reason for what they do and what they seek in life. We can never honestly know what it's like to be another person, but with careful thought and effort, we can get close. We can gain a deeper understanding of why they do what they do and what experiences in their lives have led to their current choices.

Sweet Smell of Success (1957)

Starring Burt Lancaster, Tony Curtis, Susan Harrison, Martin Milner

The Quote

J.J. HUNSECKER: *I'd hate to take a bite outta you. You're a cookie full of arsenic.*

The Context

In this noir thriller, J.J. Hunsecker is a ruthless gossip columnist whose power depends on building and destroying careers. When his younger sister starts dating a "lowly" jazz musician, he will do anything to end the relationship. He recruits Sidney Falco, a press agent who devises a devious plan to break up the couple and gain space in Hunsecker's column in return.

As Sidney executes his several unsavory schemes to separate the young couple, J.J. watches with awe at Sidney's ability to match his own unscrupulous nature. "I'd hate to take a bite outta you. You're a cookie full of arsenic" is J.J.'s way of saying, "You're not to be underestimated."

The Lesson

Give respect where respect is due.

It's enjoyable watching two legendary screen actors (who usually play the hero) engage in immoral chess games around town. Burt Lancaster plays Hunsecker, the power-hungry tyrant, and Tony Curtis plays Sidney, the barking dog begging for table scraps. Though they are cut from the same cloth, the power imbalance is immense.

J.J. rarely acknowledges Sidney, but as soon as Sidney has something he wants, J.J. is entirely attentive. Sidney's plans are complex, but he keeps the plates spinning like a seasoned performer. From him, I learned how to juggle many plates at once among multiple people over an extended period. As a producer, I constantly work with groups of people who are isolated, and I often ask myself:

What do they already know?

What should they know?
What do I need them to understand to move the project forward?
How are they reacting to this information?
What are the expectations for what happens next?

And then the process is repeated for the next person. And the next. And then back to the first person. Around and around until the main goal is achieved. Unless, of course, we're in a *Star Trek: The Next Generation* type of situation where we're always meeting around a conference table, I'm usually tracking down people in person or via video chat to find out what they know and how to get them where they need to be—just like Sidney.

When J.J. finally takes a moment to honestly look at Sidney and see the extent of his accomplishments and how far he is willing to go, he delivers a line that's both sharp and an excellent show of admiration. No one will ever fully know all I have done to support the people I work with and to achieve our mission's goals. But there are moments when someone recognizes me and appreciates what I've done, and that makes the journey worthwhile. I only wish all of them were as stylish as J.J. Hunsecker.

The Tall T (1957)

Starring Randolph Scott, Richard Boone, Maureen O'Sullivan

The Quote

PAT BRENNAN: *Some things a man can't ride around.*

The Context

Pat Brennan has been kidnapped by a gang of murderers but manages to gain the upper hand and kills one of the men. He has a chance to run but chooses to stay and finish them off once and for all, confronting them with the line, "Some things a man can't ride around." As far as he's concerned, you have to face things head-on in life, not avoid them.

The Lesson

It's essential to confront all parts of yourself and recognize how they affect your life. Any issues you encounter should be addressed directly. Avoiding them only prolongs the problem.

This film sparked a chain reaction that profoundly shaped my life. When my father was thirteen years old, he went to the cinema to see this movie. He arrived early, while the previous showing was ending, and he decided to see what happened.

The music playing as Brennan said this quote intrigued my father. He realized that music can evoke a mood and that it's just as important (if not more) than the actors. He began studying film music, learning about all of the composers and styles of the past and present. His dream was to become a film composer. He knew how to play the trombone. He was drafted into the Fifth Army Band before being sent to Vietnam for a year. When he came back, he met and married my mother, and thirteen years later, my mom was pregnant with me.

While I was still in my mother's womb, my father played film music for me all the time. When I was born, he named me after an Oscar-winning Russian-born film composer named Dimitri Tiomkin. He hoped that I would live to fulfill his dream. We watched movies all the time, but always with an ear to what the music was doing at every moment.

Much to his dismay, I became enamored with the movies themselves rather than the music. I went on to disappoint him by joining Columbia College Chicago not as a film music major but as a film producing major. I like collaboration, scheduling, and budgeting. I know how to work with a composer, but I have no interest in the actual construction of music.

As I moved out and began making my own life choices, I realized why I loved movies so much. If my father hadn't been inspired by that one moment in an obscure Randolph Scott western, I might not have been born, let alone become a major movie geek. As much as I didn't want to be like my father, I had to accept that he was a significant influence on the life I now lead. His impact, positive or inescapable, is a fact of my life. Some things a man can't ride around.

1970s and 1980s

The A-Team (1983-1987)

Starring George Peppard, Mr. T, Dirk Benedict, Dwight Schultz

The Quote

HANNIBAL: *I love it when a plan comes together!*

The Context

The A-Team is a group of ex-US Army Special Forces soldiers who were wrongly convicted of a crime and have escaped from a maximum-security stockade to the Los Angeles underground. Still wanted by the government, they are now mercenaries for hire.

Hannibal Smith, the lead planner of the A-Team, always has a plan. And when that plan succeeds, he smiles, pulls out a cigar, and says, "I love it when a plan comes together!"

The Lesson

When your plans finally click into place, pause and savor them.

Hannibal Smith is basically my spirit guide–his grin every time a plan succeeds is the energy I try to channel daily. Life is tough. Production is tougher. Relationships? A beautiful, chaotic mess. If we're going to pour ourselves into all this hard work, shouldn't we at least revel in the victories?

Think of your favorite TV or movie moment–the one that still sparks something in you. Got it? Good. Now consider everything it took to bring that moment to life. It didn't just materialize when someone hit "record." It was imagined, written, debated, pitched, funded, cast, costumed, scheduled, and endlessly prepped. A location had to be chosen. The scene needed lights, sound, direction, rehearsal, and finally that perfect take. And then came the editing, color, sound design, music, reviews, fixes, and the final export that landed in your theater.

The chain of events behind that single emotional beat is astonishing. One tiny change in the universe and it might never have existed.

Now imagine you produced it–pulled the strings, steered the chaos, shepherded the team. Standing in a theater, watching an audience react, arms crossed, smiling: "I love it when a plan comes together." Because you earned it.

In life, big or small, every plan coming together deserves that same joy.

Aliens (1986)

Starring Sigourney Weaver, Michael Biehn, Paul Reiser, Lance Henriksen, Bill Paxton, Al Matthews

The Quote

PRIVATE HUDSON: *We're on an express elevator to hell, going down!*

The Context

A group of gung-ho Marines are on a spacecraft orbiting the planet LV-426, where aliens apparently are threatening a colony from Earth. They are geared up and ready to go to war, prepared for anything–or so they think. As they load into their drop ship, as they have done for hundreds of missions, they are locked, loaded, and ready to descend into the atmosphere of a planet.

Hudson, one of the Marines, always has something comedic to say. Before they drop, he yells, "We're on an express elevator to hell, going down!"as giddy as a kid playing with his toy after school.

The Lesson

If you gotta go, go with gusto. Even a poorly executed plan can be thrilling when done with enthusiasm.

These Marines were definitely cocky. They joked during the briefing with the only expert alive on what they were facing. Their egos were sky high. And they tackled every problem with the same militaristic bravado. They quickly realized they were outmatched in every way.

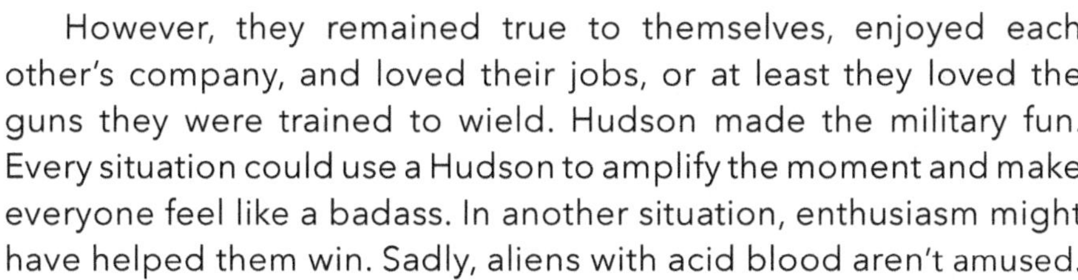

However, they remained true to themselves, enjoyed each other's company, and loved their jobs, or at least they loved the guns they were trained to wield. Hudson made the military fun. Every situation could use a Hudson to amplify the moment and make everyone feel like a badass. In another situation, enthusiasm might have helped them win. Sadly, aliens with acid blood aren't amused.

The Quote

SERGEANT APONE: *Nobody touch nothin'.*

The Context

The Marines are entering an engineering structure that is increasingly being covered in a foreign organic resin they've never seen before. As they move farther into the structure, the team's sergeant breaks the silence most hilariously by saying, "Nobody touch nothin'."

The Lesson

This was my catchphrase during the pandemic for apparent reasons. I also use it on set when everything is set just right and someone wants to go tweak the lights again.

Sometimes it is better to leave things alone and step away slowly. Or else the walls may come alive and kill you.

...And Justice for All (1979)

Starring Al Pacino, Jack Warden, John Forsythe, Lee Strasberg

The Quote

ARTHUR KIRKLAND: *They want me to defend Fleming because of my moral integrity. And if I don't defend him, they're going to have me disbarred for being unethical.*

The Context

Arthur Kirkland is a defense lawyer who is forced to defend a judge he hates. To make matters worse, he knows the judge is guilty of rape, but the system won't allow him to step down. If he defends the judge, it will send out the message that he must be innocent.

The problem is that the judge's own people are blackmailing him, meaning he doesn't have much of a choice. Years ago, he turned in a client whom he knew would commit murder, thereby breaking attorney-client confidentiality. He did the wrong thing for the right reasons, and now it's being used against him to force him to take the judge's case.

The Lesson

Life is full of contradictions and rarely makes sense. In Arthur's case, this quote perfectly sums up the dilemma. Do the wrong thing because you have moral standards, or do the right thing and be punished. They have bent the situation to fit their needs.

People can be absurd, acting both in their own self-interest and against it. This quote reminds me that some people can truly justify the contradictions they create.

I accept that the world will hardly ever make sense. The only thing I can control is myself, and sometimes even that is hard. It helps to keep investigating the choices presented in the moment. What are the motivations of the people involved? What are the ripple effects each choice will cause? Is there truly no third option? Playing chess helps.

I try to ignore what people think when it comes to making a choice. Arthur knew he had good morals despite them being used to blackmail him into an impossible choice. And in the end, he made a choice that he felt was right, no matter the consequences. Most of the time when we are stressing out about the choices we need to make, we don't realize that we have already made the choice. Lock out the noise and understand why you made the choice.

Die Hard (1988)

Starring Bruce Willis, Alan Rickman, Bonnie Bedelia

The Quote

JOHN MCCLANE: *Let's see you take THIS under advisement, jerkweed! Geronimo, Motherfucker!*

The Context

No context needed. Either you have seen *Die Hard*, or you need to see *Die Hard*.

Just kidding.

John is having a terrible day. He is fighting terrorists while arguing that the police force should be helping him. He finds himself in a position to support the good guys who are pinned down. The good news is that he was able to procure some explosives from the terrorists. The bad news is that he is so fed up that he decides not to measure the amount of explosives to use. He uses all of them, then chucks them down an elevator shaft.

The Lesson

Sometimes you have to ignore the skills you don't have, be decisive, and save the day.

This moment is the very definition of no more fucks left to give. He's pissed. He's backed into a corner, and no one is coming to help him. He's got tools but no direct knowledge of how to use them best. None of that stops him. He steps up and uses everything available (including office furniture) to save the moment. And why go little when you can blow up an entire floor of the building you are trying to save? And it works!

Ghostbusters (1984)

Starring Bill Murray, Dan Aykroyd, Harold Ramis, Ernie Hudson

The Quote

WINSTON ZEDDEMORE: *Ray, when someone asks you if you're a god, you say "YES"!*

The Context

Busting ghosts makes the Ghostbusters feel good. But they've met their match when they face off with a literal god, Gozer.

Gozer tests them by asking if they are also gods. Ray answers honestly that they aren't. Since they don't measure up to god status, Gozer then proceeds to blast them with lightning and torture them. After they recover, Winston, the voice of reason in the group, scolds Ray, "When someone asks you if you're a god, you say "YES"!

The Lesson

Fake it till you make it.

Just joking.

To be honest, I've never felt qualified for any job I've ever had. Not because I lied about my qualifications and skills, but because you can never be sure you can handle every experience you'll come across in a new role. An interview is, in many ways, a promise that you will use whatever skills you have to respond to problems you don't know you'll encounter.

During a job interview, I was asked, "What would you do if the team was behind on a project you were managing?" My answer consisted of a few steps, including talking to those involved and determining a strategy to keep things on track. I learned later that it was this answer that helped me get the job.

Do I come across situations like that in my career? More times than I can count. Do I always take those same steps? I would say it's a 50/50 split. But I do the best I can with each situation as it presents itself. More importantly, I answered the interview question with

enough confidence that I convinced the interviewers (and myself) that I could do the job.

You may not be a god, but if you project confidence in your abilities, you might just convince everyone that you are one.

The Quote

DR. RAYMOND STANTZ: *I couldn't help it. It just popped in there.*
DR. PETER VENKMAN: *What? WHAT 'just popped in there'?*

The Context

The Traveler has come to destroy the Ghostbusters and New York City, including Staten Island. Whatever enters the heads of the Ghostbusters is the form in which the Traveler will take to destroy them. Peter tells them to empty their heads. Ray cannot help himself. Something just pops in there. And he is too scared to say the words.

The Lesson

It happens all the time. We think of something we shouldn't say. We say something we don't really mean. We can't help ourselves. Open mouth (or brain) and insert foot. Saying "It just popped in there" or "What just popped in there?" in a dramatic way can help ease the tension in any situation.

The Quote

PETER VENKMAN: *I love this plan! I'm excited to be a part of it! LET'S DO IT!*

The Context

The good news: The Ghostbusters finally have a plan to save the day. The bad news: It has a slim chance of success and a high risk of killing them. But time is running out, and it's their only option. Ignoring the group's sour mood, Peter chooses to embrace the plan despite its flaws and motivates the team to get it done.

The Lesson

I love it when we can all hit the field together, even with only a rough plan. If you're sharing space with me and there's a task that needs to be completed, I guarantee we'll leave the huddle with a plan and everyone will know their role.

A bad plan is better than no plan at all. A bad plan can develop into a good plan. Sometimes a bad plan seems inadequate, but it still has a slight chance of success. It can also trigger a response that helps us learn more about the situation we face.

When dealing with group situations, I love it when we come up with a plan together. It is the best feeling in the world (second only to the taste of bacon). And when we agree on that plan, no matter how good or bad it is, I will be the first to shout.

Every plan needs a hype person, no matter how bad it is. "I love this plan! I'm excited to be a part of it!" I bring that excitement because we are taking on a situation together. And if we lose, at least we succeeded at trying together.

Innerspace (1987)

Starring Dennis Quaid, Martin Short, Meg Ryan

The Quote

LT. TUCK PENDLETON: *When things are at their darkest, pal, it's a brave man that can kick back and party.*

The Context

Tuck is part of a military science experiment in which he is shrunk down and (mistakenly) injected inside grocery clerk Jack Putter. Their journey is filled with mischief and danger as they gradually become aware of each other while being pursued by several villains. In a moment of bonding, Tuck says, "When things are at their darkest, pal, it's a brave man that can kick back and party," and literally cues the music so they can vigorously dance their troubles away.

The Lesson

Rest and recharging are also productive.

It doesn't get darker than being trapped inside another person. No matter what situation you face, a well-timed dance break can brighten the mood. Resilience is key, but we can't be "on" all the time. Taking a break to party can be refreshing and make the problem seem smaller than it was when you were laser-focused on it.

In high school and college, I was intense because I thought I had to be on duty at all times. Perched like Batman, I could stop all evil or, at the very least, push myself and my crew through anything at any time. I soon learned to relax and use my energy only when needed.

Lean on Me (1989)

Starring Morgan Freeman, Beverly Todd, Robert Guillaume, Jermaine Hopkins

The Quote

DR. FRANK NAPIER: *If you're so hot on discipline, then goddammit start by accepting mine because contrary to popular opinion, I'M THE HEAD NIGGER IN CHARGE!*

The Context

Dr. Napier is the head of the local school district. One of his schools, Eastside High, is falling apart. He hires his friend Joe Clark to be the new principal in an effort to clean up the school (literally), make it safer, and improve the test score average for the students. Joe takes drastic and dramatic steps to improve the situation. Though his efforts are having a positive impact, he also draws the ire of some of the teachers and parents.

The usually mild-mannered Frank steps back in to remind Joe that some of Joe's behavior will not be tolerated. In a beautiful yet heated monologue, Frank reminds him who is really in charge.

The Lesson

Surround yourself with friends who are fiercely honest with you.

I am blessed to have friends and family who are willing to call me out when I am way off base. The most impactful lessons I have learned have come not from classrooms or winning battles during challenging shoots and events, but from friends putting me in my place when I needed it most. We never know we need tough love until it's too late. When you realize that person said exactly what you needed to hear, you'll see that it's a relationship to cherish.

The Quote

JOE CLARK: *I don't have to do nothing but stay Black and die!*

The Context

Joe is in jail because, in his quest to help the students of Eastside High, he also broke a few rules. The students march on the jail in protest. The mayor, who was a part of the plan to jail Joe, tells him that he must tell the students to go home for their own safety. Joe fires back, "I don't have to do nothing but stay Black and die!"

The Lesson

Do only what you need to do to survive.

We are all so swamped. We have massive to-do lists that are prescribed to us by our parents, partners, work, society, tradition, or our own impatience. We get so wrapped up in the overflow of to-dos that we never stop and ask what we really need to do to truly survive.

Do we really need to buy a house and all the steps that that entails? Do we really want to be a parent, or do our own parents pressure us? Do we need to build a business, or are we just lonely and bored?

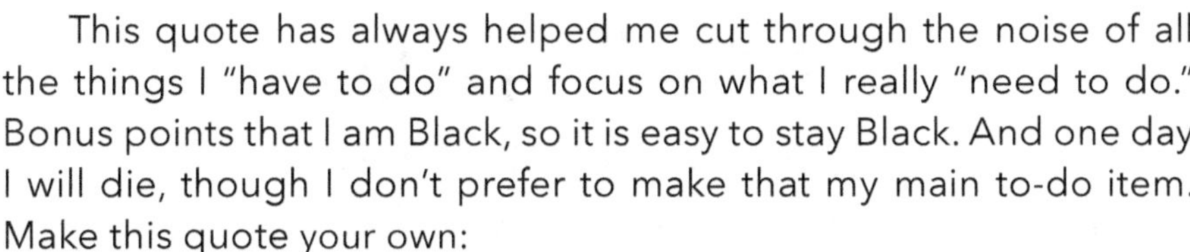

This quote has always helped me cut through the noise of all the things I "have to do" and focus on what I really "need to do." Bonus points that I am Black, so it is easy to stay Black. And one day I will die, though I don't prefer to make that my main to-do item. Make this quote your own:

- I don't have to do nothing but eat and play video games!
- I don't have to do nothing but build this shed and jog!
- I don't have to do nothing but write this book and watch movies!

It helps to find the bare minimum of what you need to do. Striving for more is essential. But when you are stressed, take stock of what is most important.

The Quote

THOMAS SAMS: *We don't want a good principal! We want Mr. Clark!*

The Context

The students of Eastside High are marching on city hall because their aggressive but caring principal is behind bars. The head of the parents' group is trying to force him out of the job because she disagrees with his methods. In a tense standoff, she tells the students they could get a better principal.

One student, Thomas Sams, was almost kicked out when Joe Clark started. Mr. Clark decided to take a chance on him and let him come back to school. During the standoff, he definitively stands up and screams, "We don't want a good principal! We want Mr. Clark!" to which the massive crowd of students agrees.

The Lesson

Better doesn't always mean good.

M.A.S.K. (1986)

Season 2, Episode 4: The Battle of the Giants

Starring (voices) Doug Stone, Brendan McKane, Sharon Noble, Mark Halloran, Graeme McKenna

The Quote

MATT TRAKKER: *Perfect in its simplicity, and the one plan they'll never guess: the no-plan plan.*

The Context

Matt Trakker is the head of an anti-terrorist organization called M.A.S.K. Armed with transforming vehicles, they are continuously challenged by and thwarting the efforts of the evil Venom. In this particular scene, Matt and his team are trying to figure out their next move when Matt determines that having no plan might be the way to go.

The Lesson

I use this quote constantly because there are moments when we really need a plan but one just doesn't exist. My all-famous "no-plan plan" is a humorous way of saying we will wing it. But even then, I am still developing a plan. It's like oxygen—I'm always planning.

Masters of the Universe (1987)

Starring Dolph Lundgren, Frank Langella, Courteney Cox

The Quote

SKELETOR: *I ache to smash you out of existence! To drive your cursed face from my memories forever!*

The Context

After years of fierce combat between their forces, He-Man and Skeletor are finally face-to-face. Skeletor is exasperated from his many failed attempts to kill his foe. They exchange words before their weapons clash, and Skeletor tells He-Man exactly what he thinks of him.

The Lesson

If you are going to be angry, curse your enemy with style and humor.

Ever have that one person who bothers you so much you truly want to erase them from existence? If so, this would be a great line to use in an everyday context.

Predator (1987)

Starring Arnold Schwarzenegger, Carl Weathers, Jesse Ventura, Elpidia Carrillo, Bill Duke

The Quote

MAC: *You're ghostin' us, motherfucker. I don't care who you are back in the world, you give away our position one more time, I'll bleed you, real quiet, and leave ya here–got that?*

The Context

An elite military team is traversing the jungle on a rescue mission. The equivalent of a military politician with an ulterior motive joins them. His duplicity is causing friction, and his inexperience is giving away their position. So one of the team members decides to confront him with this line.

The Lesson

Know your surroundings. Know your role. Be honest.

If you are the experienced person in the room, look after your less experienced colleagues. I am not an advocate of threats. I have, from time to time, pulled someone aside on set when they weren't performing well. I always ask them what is going on from their perspective, then I present my perspective in an effort to kindly yet directly help them understand how their behavior is affecting others and the work at hand. Then we work together to find a way to adjust and improve the situation.

If you are the inexperienced person in the room, it helps to acknowledge it. Some people really don't belong in certain situations. They try to blend in, but it's not their natural habitat. Be honest with yourself. Watch those around you and do your best to learn from them. Read the room and ask questions if the moment allows.

RoboCop (1987)

Starring Peter Weller, Nancy Allen, Dan O'Herlihy, Ronny Cox

The Quote

THE OLD MAN: *Nice shootin', son. What's your name?*

ROBOCOP: *Murphy.*

The Context

Alex Murphy is a Detroit police officer who was killed in the line of duty and rebuilt as the cybernetic crimefighter, RoboCop. To ensure the man and the machine were compatible, the company that built him, OCP, erased his memory. They didn't do the perfect job though, as throughout his journey, he still experiences flashes of his old identity. At the end, when the head of OCP congratulates him for saving his own life, he asks RoboCop his name. He responds with his human name, "Murphy," smiles, and walks out. Cue the credits.

The Lesson

Identity is a choice.

This movie holds a special place in my heart. It was the first film I saw in a theater. I was six years old. My father and I watched it in the theater eleven times. I never get tired of it. When it was about to end, and the Old Man asked his name, I always thought he would say "RoboCop." I remember people in the theater exclaiming "RoboCop" out loud during the pause between the question and the answer.

The journey prepares us for the character to transform physically and emotionally from Murphy to RoboCop, and ultimately to an evolved version of RoboCop by the end of the movie. But he actually managed to override his programming and reconnect with his human self while living with his cybernetic enhancements.

This simple yet powerful moment taught me that no matter our experiences and their impact on us, only we can define our identity. No parent, partner, or evil multibillion-dollar corporation can tell us who we are. Influences on who we should be and what we should care about bombard us daily. And we have no control over the people we meet or how they will influence us, nor over the random world events that occur.

What we do have control over is what we decide to do with each moment in our lives, what we believe, and what we care about. All those choices shape who we are, and we can even contradict ourselves. Even that is a choice we hold in our power.

I'm not suggesting we have to announce our identity in every room we enter. We should feel confident that no matter the place or situation, we remain true to ourselves. However, there are crucial moments when we need to take a stand and, through our choices or words, reveal our true selves.

Remember to think first, stay authentic, smile, and leave a lasting impression. You never know–perhaps a young six-year-old is watching and will be inspired by you for years to come.

Rocky II (1979)

Starring Sylvester Stallone, Talia Shire, Burgess Meredith, Burt Young

The Quote

MICKEY GOLDMILL: *Get that olive oil out of ya!*

The Context

Boxer Rocky Balboa, or "Rocky," is training to win. His gym trainer, Mickey, has inspired generations of boxers like Rocky with his no-nonsense, tough-love approach. As he shouts, "Get that olive oil out of ya!" his assistant is slapping Rocky's stomach as hard as he can while he's doing sit-ups.

The Lesson

Use whatever you have to encourage someone to do their best.

This quote is part Italian slur, part encouragement, but it stuck with me. Mickey calls Rocky a "greasy I-talian tank" among many other slurs that would be-off color today. But the image of olive oil coursing through Rocky's veins and joints and him sweating it out is unforgettable. It was a random line they probably caught in a string of shouts on set, but I feel it was this moment where Rocky went from trying to *doing*.

The people we know and love need all types of encouragement to make it through the day. While I am not an advocate of racial slurs as encouragement, I am in favor of doing whatever it takes to reach a level of camaraderie that makes you comfortable with encouraging your mates. Push them to keep going, keep fighting, and keep living.

Rocky III (1982)

Starring Sylvester Stallone, Talia Shire, Mr. T, Burt Young, Carl Weathers, Burgess Meredith

The Quote

ADRIAN: *What do we have that can't be replaced? What? A house. We got cars, we've got money! We got everything but the truth. What's the truth, dammit?!*

The Context

Rocky is in training for his fight with Clubber Lang, but his heart and his head are not focused. His wife, Adrian, is usually meek and shy, but she takes this moment to figuratively grab him by the collar and force him to admit why he is hesitating. She systematically breaks down each of his arguments and excuses until she finally gets him to accept the truth. He is afraid.

The Lesson

Be your own Adrian.

Admit it. We all add layers and layers of bullshit on top of the real emotions that are holding us back. Rather than face the truth, we make excuses, blame others, and try to fix every other problem but the main one we are facing. Fear is usually the lowest common denominator among all issues, and yet it is the most complicated emotion to admit. We are afraid of our fear.

We all need an Adrian in our lives. Someone who is not afraid to call us out, strip away the layers, and force us to admit what we've been avoiding. It can sound mean, but when there is trust and love, it can be precisely what we need.

I have three very close friends who are like brothers, each in their own way holding me down like a fox caught in a trap and holding up a mirror to my soul. I do the same for them. And it is all from a place of love. No matter how much we dig into each other, we know at the end of it that we all want the same thing: for each of us to grow.

When you don't have an Adrian around, you have to call yourself out. It helps to be aware of your emotions and the reasons behind them. I find that the Five Whys is a helpful technique when talking to yourself. It's literally where you continue asking why and will most likely get to the real reason. For example:

1. Why am I acting like this? Because I am angry.
2. Why am I angry? Because I feel ignored.
3. Why do I feel ignored? Because my friend is focused on someone else.
4. Why are they focused on someone else? Because they want to develop another friendship.
5. Why does their other friendship bother me? Because I am afraid of being abandoned.

Only then can you take steps to address the reason you're afraid rather than spinning like a top in the surface-level anger. To grow, you must be open to digging beneath the surface of your reactions and uncover the truth.

Rocky and Adrian had everything they could ever want except the truth. If she hadn't stepped up, he wouldn't have had another epic training montage, and he would have been destroyed in the ring. Admitting his fear helped him develop the skills and resilience to face it.

Spaceballs (1987)

Starring Mel Brooks, John Candy, Rick Moranis, Bill Pullman, Daphne Zuniga

The Quote

LONE STAR: *Take only what you need to survive.*

The Context

Space cowboy Lone Star and his partner, Barf, have just rescued Princess Vespa in their Winnebago spaceship. As they make their escape, the ship runs out of gas, and they crash land on a deserted planet.

Desperate to find water and shelter, they decide to leave the ship. But the princess throws a fit when she can't take her luggage with her. Lone Star, fed up with her attitude, issues the command, "Take only what you need to survive."

The Lesson

We carry way too much "stuff" with us from one place to another. From the possessions in our homes to the items in our backpacks, we could stand to carry fewer things. Take a moment and look at your bag, your suitcase, or the room you're sitting in. I guarantee there are items in your view that you could do without.

When I'm packing for a trip or a video shoot, I take only what I need to survive. I'm usually an advocate of "I'd rather have it than not need it," but there is a fine line between being prepared and overpacking.

The same applies to emotional baggage. We carry a lot of the past with us. Usually, our bags are filled with our mistakes, fears from past events, and old acquaintances. Take a moment to look into your soul. Seriously, close your eyes and notice the first thoughts that come to your mind.

I guarantee some of those thoughts hold feelings and ideas based on past regrets. While we desire positivity and catharsis, we can fall into the trap of berating ourselves for moments long gone.

We can be our own harshest critics. It helps to take inventory of these memories and decide which ones are worth carrying.

I am not a fan of making New Year's resolutions. It's often impossible to commit to something for a full year. Life happens. Things change our priorities every day. Leading up to the new year, I make a list of all aspects of my life—projects, events, relationships, priorities, goals, and more. Everything that has mattered over the years goes on that list.

Then I meditate on the list for a week or two and deeply consider what I actually want to take with me into the new year. Almost every time, the second list ends up being one-fifth of the original list. I realize that I am carrying so many things that I no longer need to worry about. Those items were essential at one point but no longer bring me any value.

At the start of the year, I promise myself to hold onto only what's important, and I leave the rest in the past, never to bother me again. If they reappear in my mind, I am quickly reminded of my promise and gently let go of it again. We are fragile beings and need to declutter our spaces and our minds so we can move forward into whatever comes next.

The Quote

BARF: *I'm a mawg: half man, half dog. I'm my own best friend!*

The Context

Lone Star's sidekick, Barf, introduces himself.

The Lesson

Be your own best friend.

I love my friends and family, but I enjoy different things than they do and have often found myself having to go it alone and be my own best friend. And why not? I know what I want and when I like it, and I'm determined enough to take care of myself. I grew up as an only child with working parents, so I spent a lot of time on my own. To this day, I find time to go to movies, roam around town, and go to restaurants by myself. This book was written in a moment when I was by myself. I have fundamentally found a way to replace loneliness with the feeling that I am the only person on every step of this life journey.

There is only one mawg, and I am not him. But I am me, and I am all I need.

The Transformers: The Movie (1986)

Starring (voices) Judd Nelson, Leonard Nimoy, Eric Idle, Orson Welles

The Quote

SPRINGER: *I've got better things to do tonight than die.*

The Context

The heroic Autobots are being pursued across the universe by the evil Decepticons and a planet-sized foe called Unicron. Gearing up for the fight, the Autobots transform their city into a fortress. One of the Autobots, Springer, makes a declaration as they dig in for the brutal battle: "I've got better things to do tonight than die."

The Lesson

Always be resilient.

Taking a stand against insurmountable odds is every kid's dream and most adults' nightmare. Whether it's showing up for a friend or saving the entire world, resilience is the one skill everyone needs. Very few things come easily or go according to plan. We can apply for one hundred jobs and fail to get an interview ninety-nine times. We can date 523 people and only on the 524th find what we are looking for.

One thing is for sure: Until the day we die, we are not going to die. So we should stand up and keep going until we find what we are looking for. Psych yourself up and make a clear goal for what you need to accomplish today, tonight or right now. We stress ourselves out by trying to survive a decade or a lifetime when we

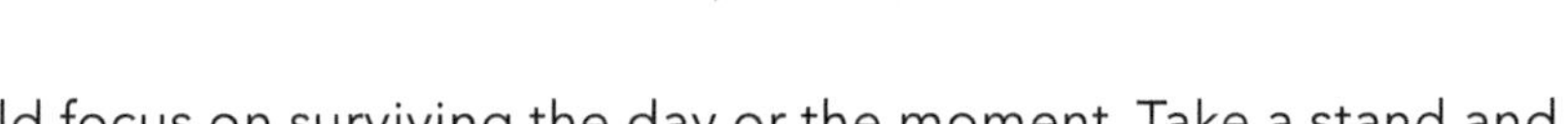

should focus on surviving the day or the moment. Take a stand and do what you can to survive the night.

If the idea of dying is too morbid or dramatic for you, feel free to modify it however you like:

- I've got better things to do tonight than fail.
- I've got better things to do tonight than lose.
- I've got better things to do tonight than miss.
- I've got better things to do tonight than give up.
- I've got better things to do tonight than lose my cool.
- I've got better things to do tonight than betray my friends.
- I've got better things to do tonight than betray myself.

When in doubt, stand across from your literal foe (e.g., a person standing in your way) or your metaphysical foe (e.g., procrastination, red tape) and utter the immortal words of Autobot leader Optimus Prime:

"One shall stand; one shall fall."

1990s

The American President (1995)

Starring Michael Douglas, Annette Bening,
Martin Sheen, Michael J. Fox

The Quote

PRESIDENT ANDREW SHEPHERD: *America isn't easy. America is advanced citizenship. You gotta want it bad, 'cause it's gonna put up a fight. It's gonna say, "You want free speech? Let's see you acknowledge a man whose words make your blood boil, who's standing center stage and advocating at the top of his lungs that which you would spend a lifetime opposing at the top of yours."*

The Context

Andrew Shepherd is the president and a widower trying to make changes to his personal life by dating a lobbyist, Sydney Ellen Wade. He is under the impression that he can keep his personal life separate from his public and political life. When he is proven wrong, he takes to the stage to admonish his political rival, Senator Bob Rumson, who demonizes Shepherd's administration using Sydney as a prop.

In part of his speech, Shepherd takes a moment to explain the true meaning of free speech, which all Americans are meant to enjoy and endure.

The Lesson

As humans, we get so entrenched in the ideas we subscribe to that we forget that everyone should have the same rights. Ourselves, our homes, our communities, our cities, and our countries all have belief systems. And when we find like-minded people, we believe that our beliefs are right, and in some way, intentional or unintentional, we think everyone else is misguided.

This quote reminds us that the same free speech we enjoy comes at the cost of having to listen to another person's free speech. Even if you feel that person is wrong in every way, they have the same right to speak as you do, and it's incorrect to silence any opinion just because we disagree with it.

If we all spent more time listening to each other and less time trying to shout the other side down, we would learn more about ourselves and continuously find common ground. Humanity is an experiment that is constantly evolving. When we listen and acknowledge each other as much as we would want the same, we all can win.

Another 48 Hrs. (1990)

Starring Eddie Murphy, Nick Nolte

The Quote

REGGIE HAMMOND: *I HAVE BEEN HAVING A VERY BAD DAY! I just got out of jail this morning! Already I've been shot at, I was on a bus that flipped over seventeen times, bitch tried to stab me in the bathroom, and somebody blew up my Porsche!*

The Context

Reggie Hammond has just been released from prison and is reluctantly working with Jack Cates to find a dangerous criminal. Along the way, they have a few … setbacks. Jack finds himself in a bar fight. At first, he has the upper hand, and Reggie is enjoying the show. As soon as the tide turns against Jack, Reggie grabs a gun, shoots three warning shots, stops the fight, and then lists off the tragic (and hilarious) events that have taken place that day.

The Lesson

Say it to survive it.

This scene is hilarious because you can hear how much pain Reggie's in as he lists every item. In any other situation, you would assume he was exaggerating, but we, the audience, know everything he says is true.

We all have bad days, but sometimes we hold on to them way too tightly. It helps just to get it off your chest, to yell as loud as you can to the heavens all the things that are bothering you. Get it out. You can talk to your partner, your friend, your therapist, a room full of people who want to kick your ass, or even to a mirror. After putting it into words, it might not seem so bad (unless your Porsche is actually obliterated), or you could then plot a course back to better times. Even Reggie realized he needed Jack to get through the mess he was in.

Any Given Sunday (1999)

Starring Al Pacino, Cameron Diaz, Jamie Foxx

The Quote

TONY D'AMATO: *I fight for you 'til the day I die.*

The Context

Tony is the coach of the legendary Miami Sharks football team. His star, yet aging, quarterback has just exited the game due to a massive back injury. Aware that the quarterback worries someone younger is going to take his job, Tony reassures him by saying, "I fight for you 'til the day I die." And he means it.

The Lesson

The good ones are worth fighting for.

I've worked with some fantastic people. Folks who care so much about the project, the product, their own growth, or the development of those around them that you can't help but defend them. I call it the "Dimitri Protection Plan." Any way I can support them, I will. When I say, "I fight for you 'til the day I die," I mean it. Everyone I work with gets this treatment.

There are a few people for whom I have a special quote (you know who you are). I tell them, "You call. I come. It's that simple." This means that no matter where I am in the world, when you need

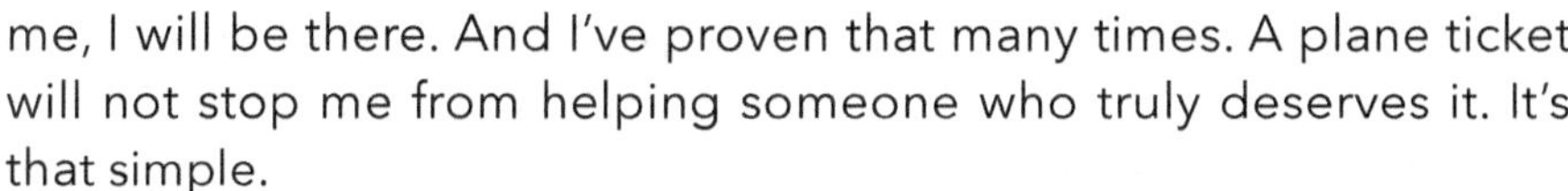

me, I will be there. And I've proven that many times. A plane ticket will not stop me from helping someone who truly deserves it. It's that simple.

The Quote

TONY D'AMATO: *You're a goddamn quarterback! You know what that means? It's the top spot, kid. It's the guy who takes the fall. It's the guy everybody's looking at first—the leader of a team—who will support you when they understand you. Who will break their ribs and their noses and their necks for you, because they believe. 'Cause you make them believe. That's a quarterback.*

The Context

When both Tony's veteran and backup Miami Sharks quarterbacks get injured, he is forced to rely on the young, talented yet inexperienced Willie Beaman to lead the team.

As Willie's star begins to rise, the team suffers because of his selfishness. In an effort to foster leadership, Tony invites Willie over for dinner. Their already strained relationship deteriorates further when Willie expresses the opinion that Tony is too old and that the game should be played Willie's way. Tony responds with his thoughts on what it truly means to be a team leader.

The Lesson

A true leader sets the tone for the team.

This is the ultimate definition of what it takes to be a leader. It is not always about flashing lights and glamour. It requires sacrifice and understanding for people to trust the person at the top. Saying you are a leader doesn't make it so. It takes hard work, dedication, and resilience, and only when they see how much you care about the team and the mission will people trust you to lead.

I have been blessed over the years to lead many teams into creative battles. As a producer I focus on the people as much as, or more than, the product we are making. It takes people to create, and if you know the people, you know what you need to do to help each of them succeed. The project or product is also important, as it's the reason we come together to achieve our personal goals.

When the team forms, I start by understanding where each person is and where they want to be. Why are they on this project? What do they hope to accomplish, both on this battlefield and in their career overall? What makes them tick? What do they need to get through a tough day? How do they respond to praise and criticism? Producing is, in many ways, a short-term equivalent of being a therapist.

And I say that with great respect for the years of hard work and practice it takes to be an actual therapist.

Back to producing. With all that information about who they are and what they want, I do everything possible to help the team feel seen and supported. I am the first to arrive on set and the last to leave. I care about how they are coming to and from the set, I'm open to hearing what's affecting them outside the set so they don't feel alone and can focus on the project at hand. My not-so-secret weapon is ensuring everyone is fed and has food, which makes them feel appreciated.

On a deeper level, I show them that I am willing to do whatever it takes to complete the project without sacrificing the team. I will help in other roles if someone needs to step out for a phone call or a break. I'll rush-order tools or parts if it helps them get the job done. I even took off my shirt and gave it to a presenter who was sweating heavily, then went to the store and bought more T-shirts so we could refresh him throughout the day.

When you care, people see it in their own ways and reciprocate by dedicating themselves to the project, each other, or both. The sacrifices of leaders give the team permission to care and the trust to bring their true selves to the room.

Apollo 13 (1995)

Starring Tom Hanks, Bill Paxton, Kevin Bacon, Gary Sinise

The Quote

JACK SWIGERT: *Farewell, Aquarius, and we thank you.*

The Context

Three astronauts are on their way to the moon. The mission encounters a catastrophic failure and is forced to abandon its efforts to land on the moon in favor of surviving the trip home. Their vehicle comes in two parts: the Command Module, called Odyssey, and the Lunar Module, Aquarius. Odyssey was supposed to fly them to and from the moon, but it became damaged en route. Aquarius was designed to land only on the moon, but has now become a lifeboat–their only hope of returning to Earth.

When they miraculously reach Earth's atmosphere, they return to the Odyssey (which has the necessary heat shield for reentry)and cut Aquarius loose. As their galactic lifeboat floats away, they take one last look at the module that kept them alive. One of the astronauts, Jack Swigert, says, "Farewell, Aquarius, and we thank you."

The Lesson

Honor the space in which you create.

Spaces have a soul. I've produced in lots of spaces, including homes, classrooms, abandoned buildings, performance centers, stages, restaurants, bank vaults, and rooftops. You name it, and I have probably produced something in it. When making content, it can feel like you and your team are fighting a small war. But that war has to take place somewhere.

In film school we were taught to leave a location in better condition than when we found it. That's because the area in which you are filming is as important as the people you are sharing that space with. You have to find the right space for the content you are filming. You have to prepare the space for the project. You have to survive the filming of that project and then clean up, preparing it for its next inhabitants.

Upon loading out after a shoot, I always take a moment to turn back and honor the space by saying, "Farewell, *insert space name*, and we thank you. Thank you for housing us. Thank you for bringing us together. Thank you for being our creative space. Thank you for keeping us safe. Thank you for being a part of our journey."

Back to the Future Part III (1990)

Starring Michael J. Fox, Christopher Lloyd, Mary Steenburgen

The Quote

OLD TIMER #2 (ZEKE): *Here's to ya, blacksmith.*

OLD TIMER #3 (JEB): *And to the future!*

OLD TIMER #1 (LEVI): *Amen.*

The Context

Doc Brown built a time machine and was accidentally sent back to 1885, where he fulfilled his dream of becoming a locksmith in the Old West. Typically, his policy is to not disturb the space-time continuum by keeping details of the future a secret. But the night before he's meant to go back to the future, he experiences heartbreak. He goes to the local bar frequented by three Old Timers and proceeds to tell them everything about the future.

The next morning, his partner, Marty, enters the bar and convinces Doc that they have to leave. He agrees, and the Old Timers salute him and the future.

The Lesson

Our journey into the future is not yet written, but every moment can be celebrated as if it were.

This moment became a call-and-response between my best friend and me. Almost every time we have parted over the last twenty years, one of us says, "Here's to ya, blacksmith." The other instinctively says, "And to the future!" and then we both simultaneously reply with a satisfying "Amen." It feels instinctual and natural. It's even fun when people who know us try to join the ritual.

We all want to belong to something–some kind of community–to share moments and have inside jokes. This friendship is mine. I met Spence in my first college film class. We didn't connect at first, but ended up on the same bus because we lived near each other. Once we talked, we quickly became friends and cinematic comrades. Of the many things we have in common and the rituals we have developed, this one is my favorite.

Not only is it a great call-and-response, but now that we are actually in the future of our friendship, and we were actually toasting too. It calms me to know that my choice of friend was the right one. That we can talk to each other after a three-month break as if we've been talking every day. We have the most ridiculous movie debates, as well as talk through real-life trauma. He has encouraged me to watch about a third of the movies quoted in this book. He has opened my eyes to Aerosmith, Firefly, and Mass Effect (games take much longer for me). I am thankful to have a friend like Spence and that we have such a simple repeatable ritual to remind us of our past and to look forward to the future.

Bad Boys (1995)

Starring Will Smith, Martin Lawrence

The Quote

MIKE LOWREY: *My shit always works sometimes!*

The Context

Miami police officers Mike Lowrey and Marcus Burnett are gearing up for the final fight in their effort to recover $100 million worth of confiscated heroin stolen from station headquarters. They have a daring plan to surprise the bad guys, involving a dump truck. As they prepare to attack, Mike hypes up the other officers by shouting, "My shit always works sometimes!"

The Lesson

No matter your battle cry, say it with confidence!

In any situation, confidence is key. It helps to have a plan and ensure that everyone is aware of the plan and their part in it. It is also helpful to be aware that the plans will not always work.

I remembered this quote as "My plan always works sometimes!" as I probably saw the profanity-free TV safe version the first time. With that, I see it as a hilarious way of acknowledging the contradictions that happen when we plan. It is a way to cover the spread but make people think they have a chance at winning.

Batman Forever (1995)

Starring Val Kilmer, Nicole Kidman, Chris O'Donnell, Jim Carrey, Tommy Lee Jones

The Quote

THE RIDDLER: *Your entrance was good. His was better. The difference: Showmanship!*

The Context

Edward Nygma, a.k.a. The Riddler, is throwing a party showcasing his newest invention. His partner-in-crime, Harvey "Two-Face" Dent, crashes the party with his thugs to spread some "mayhem and chaos." Nygma chides him that had they coordinated their approach, they could have "pre-sold the movie rights" to the caper. Two-Face is not phased.

All of a sudden, Batman crashes through the ceiling, and Nygma delivers the line, "Your entrance was good. His was better. The difference: Showmanship!" Batman swiftly dispatches the bad guys and kisses (or is kissed by) the femme fatale, Dr. Chase Meridian.

The Lesson

Give credit where credit is due.

Nygma and Two-Face each hated Batman and Bruce Wayne (spoiler!), but even they had to acknowledge that, like Dumbledore, Batman's got style. There isn't a villain or skylight in Gotham that doesn't fear him. And everyone knows it.

Think of someone in your life with a well-placed sense of style, and take a moment to step back and appreciate all the things that came together to create such a magical moment. Your stylish friend may be too busy being awesome to hear your praise, but give it a try anyway.

The Big Hit (1998)

Starring Mark Wahlberg, Lou Diamond Phillips, Christina Applegate

The Quote

CISCO: *Well, ain't that a bitch ...*

The Context

Assassin team member Cisco has been trying to beat his former partner, Melvin, the entire day. He engineered a kidnapping that goes wrong, betrays his friends to save his own life, and never gets to enjoy the ransom money. What should have been a normal day for an assassin who wanted to buy a boat and retire ends with his own knife in his chest.

The Lesson

Some days, nothing will go your way. Stop. Step back. Say, "Well, ain't that a bitch ... and try again tomorrow.

My wife, Naomi, is an expert at this. Besides her being one of the most caring and sympathetic people I know, one of her superpowers is her ability to shake things off and move forward.

In our fifteen years (and counting) together, we've had our share of ups and downs. Thankfully, more ups than downs. But when those down moments happen, she feels them, and then, in the span of a minute or if someone enters the room or if she shifts from one space to another, she manages to leave that feeling behind and be the best host, friend, and partner she can be for the next person she encounters.

The best part is that she never gives up. She perseveres. She keeps trying to help every person she meets find the support and connections they need. As I write this, she's chatting with at least ten other people, working to help them get what they need. When things don't quite go her way, she has her own way of saying, "Well, ain't that a bitch ..." and then continues to make magic happen.

The Quote

CISCO: *Knuckle up, bitch!*

MELVIN SMILEY: *Yeah, let's go motherfucker! Let's work.*

The Context

Cisco has been trying to kill his former partner, Melvin, all day in an effort to save his own life. Our hero Melvin keeps narrowly escaping each attempt on his life. Now they face each other man-to-man for the final showdown where only one will survive.

The Lesson

Every time I am about to handle a task, whether it's writing an email, creating a call sheet, or running a set, I tell my invisible enemy, "Knuckle up, bitch! Let's go motherfucker. Let's work!"

It started as a way to hype myself up on the first day of school. I loved going because it was my only social interaction and a chance to prove my excellence. Summer breaks were tough because I was home all the time doing chores, playing music, or hiding behind my TV. It was boring, and I constantly had to navigate my father's anger. The first day of school always felt like the start of a fun war to win.

As I grew older, the stakes got higher through college, projects, and real jobs. But the hype this quote gives me still makes the challenges fun. Imagine standing in front of your infant son, lying on his back on the changing table. His diaper is full of pee, and he's about to have a blowout poo. What better way to get through the madness than by internally yelling, "Let's go motherfucker. Let's work!" It worked every time.

The Boondock Saints (1999)

Starring Sean Patrick Flanery, Norman Reedus

The Quote

PAUL SMECKER: *Fuck! I hate cold crime scenes!*

The Context

FBI Agent Paul Smecker is highly skilled at analyzing crime scenes. He can examine the entire scene and detail exactly what happened step by step. However, he faces his challenge when dealing with brothers Connor and Murphy, who are unlike the typical Mafia thugs he usually investigates. The police assigned to work with him believe that some of the crime scenes they hear about are not connected to the current string of crimes they are investigating.

But the Connor and Murphy case couldn't be more connected to the others. Agent Smecker and his fellow officers arrive at the crime scene much later than usual when the clues he needs are harder for him to read. Due to the unconventional nature of the evidence, Smecker loses his composure and shouts, "Fuck! I hate cold crime scenes!"

The Lesson

Trust the facts, not assumptions.

The Quote

CONNOR: *Well, name one thing you're gonna need this stupid fucking rope for.*

The Context

Connor and Murphy are killing really bad people. They stumble upon an armory filled with all the guns they can think of, plus a reel of rope. Connor wants the rope, but Murphy teases him because there's no reason to need it. In a funny twist, the rope ends up being useful.

The Lesson

I would rather have something and not need it than need something and not have it—every time.

The Quote

PAUL SMECKER: *There was a firefight!*

The Context

Agent Smecker has just arrived at a crime scene. Bodies and blood are everywhere. He breaks down what happened step-by-step as we watch the brothers and their accomplice take down a room full of bad guys. As they exit the house, they are confronted by a legendary assassin.

In the climax of Smecker's recreation, he screams, "There was a firefight!" with all the passion he can muster. As he gets caught up in the reenactment of the firefight, he pulls out his own weapon and fires into the air in an orgasmic chorus of gunfire.

The Lesson

Passion can be fun.

I worked for the college I attended. One of my roles was as a tour guide for parents and students during orientation. I was constantly asked, "How do I know if I'm in the right major?" in one way or another. My answer was always the same: "If you can do that thing you think you want to do for hours on end without a break or distraction, then that is your passion."

Obviously, breaks are essential, and obsession is dangerous. But the point still stands: If you find something you love and are good at it, follow that path. I hope one day you can stand inside your own brilliance and, metaphorically, scream to the heavens and fire off a firearm with all the passion you can muster. Because then everything you sacrificed will make sense, and you'll be able to enjoy your hard work, like Agent Smecker.

Contact (1997)

Starring Jodie Foster, Matthew McConaughey, John Hurt

The Quote

S.R. HADDEN: *First rule in government spending: Why build one when you can have two at twice the price?*

The Context

Humanity receives a mysterious message revealing that we are not alone in the universe. The message contains blueprints for a machine of unknown purpose. The government builds it, but on the eve of its activation, it is destroyed by a terrorist. An eccentric billionaire, S.R. Hadden, appears and explains that a secret second machine was being made the entire time, and it is time to see what it can do.

The Lesson

Always have a backup plan!

As a producer it's always essential to have a backup plan. When I create a production schedule, I pad it with an extra hour. When I prepare a production budget, I always include a contingency. When I commission a special prop, I have two made. When I hire someone, I keep a backup person in mind. Everyone on set has a backup role, so anyone can step into another's spot, because life happens. Even when I cook I prepare more food than necessary in case additional people show up.

Unexpected events occur constantly. I believe in maintaining balance. Never enter a room without a plan. Never expect everything to go exactly as planned. Weather changes, mechanical failures happen, time estimates can be off, and sometimes people just plain suck.

Although I don't like to overspend, I do keep a backup phone case because it's an essential part of my gear. If you have billions of dollars, like S.R. Hadden, you might as well have an insurance plan. If something is vital, have another ready to use.

Crimson Tide (1995)

Starring Denzel Washington, Gene Hackman, George Dzundza

The Quote

CAPT. RAMSEY: *You knew to shut up and enjoy the view. Most eggheads want to talk it away. Your stock just went up a couple of points.*

The Context

Submarine Captain Ramsey is the old dog who doesn't need to learn new tricks. He follows orders, and when he gives them, he expects and demands they be followed. His new executive officer, Commander Hunter, was taught to understand why those orders were given. They couldn't be more different. On their maiden voyage together, they take a moment to view the sunset before the submarine submerges.

Ramsey makes a passing comment that he loves moments like this. Hunter stays silent. Ramsey praises the fact that Hunter stayed silent and let the moment play out so he could truly enjoy it.

The Lesson

Stop trying so hard and enjoy the moment.

There are two types of people: those who can read the room and those who are oblivious to it. Those who can read the room can understand the emotions of the people in it and ride that wave. I am one of those people. I don't always know what's behind the emotion of the room, and I especially don't always do the right thing, but I'm sensitive to the energy of it. And I especially have moments when I would like to enjoy the silence of the moment, like Ramsey.

Then there's the other type: those who always feel they have to do or say something. They can't let silence stand. They have to fill the moment with their thoughts constantly. What they think is the only thing that matters. My father was this way. He hated silence, especially during an argument. If you were silent, even for a moment, the argument would continue and morph into a new battleground.

For a while, I was like this. Not in speech but more in action. I always had to be doing something. If I were idle, I would have to get up and make something happen. Always be fixing. Always be working. Always be doing. It took a monumental amount of stress one day to teach me how to embrace the calm moments. I learned the power of silent contemplation. I knew the benefits of being my own peacemaker rather than burning myself out for everyone else's peace.

Whenever I meet a potential collaborator, team member, or friend, I internally give them the Ramsey test. Can they allow an enjoyable and peaceful moment to play out, or is their instinct to talk it away? I can work with both types of people. It helps me to know who I am sharing space with so I can manage my own peaceful expectations.

For myself, I had to learn how to stop trying so hard to move forward all the time and just enjoy being who I am in the present.

Dick Tracy (1990)

Starring Warren Beatty, Madonna, Al Pacino, Dustin Hoffman

The Quote

BIG BOY CAPRICE: *Wait a minute! Wait. I'm having a thought. Oh, yes. Oh, yes. I'm gonna have a thought. It's coming … It's gone.*

The Context

Crime boss Big Boy Caprice is consolidating power. And to inspire his troops, he constantly quotes the likes of Abraham Lincoln and Thomas Jefferson. Every once in a while, he is on the edge of something profound and then just loses the thought.

The Lesson

We all get lost sometimes.

This quote comes to mind constantly. It has happened at least a hundred times while writing this book. I've almost got the answer or the point, and it just floats away, never to be remembered again. In many ways, this quote is the reason I write things down as soon as they come into my brain.

As a producer, the last thing I want to do is trust my memory. There are just too many things going on and too much at stake to feed my ego by trusting everything to memory. If you tell me something is supposed to happen on a particular date, it is already in the calendar before the conversation is finished. I'm in the shower or in bed, and a profound thought strikes me, I stop the water or throw off the covers (much to my wife's dismay), and head to my nearest device to either jot it down or voice record it so that I can capture the complete integrity of the thought in its purest form.

Always have something to capture your profound ideas before they are gone. Once you move on to the following thousand thoughts, you'll never get that special one back again.

The Quote

BIG BOY CAPRICE: *What's the matter, you bums forgot how to kill people? Doesn't your work mean anything to you anymore? Have you no sense of pride in what you do? No sense of duty, no sense of destiny? I'm looking for generals; what do I got? Foot soldiers! I want Dick Tracy dead!*

The Context

Big Boy is fed up with Dick Tracy constantly surviving his cunning traps. He blames everything on his "foot soldiers."

The Lesson

Entertainers do not always make the best leaders.

Not only is this one of the first movies I saw in a movie theater, but it is also my first Al Pacino performance! I loved his acting (or overacting) from the start. He is an engaging and entertaining performer, one of my all-time favorites!

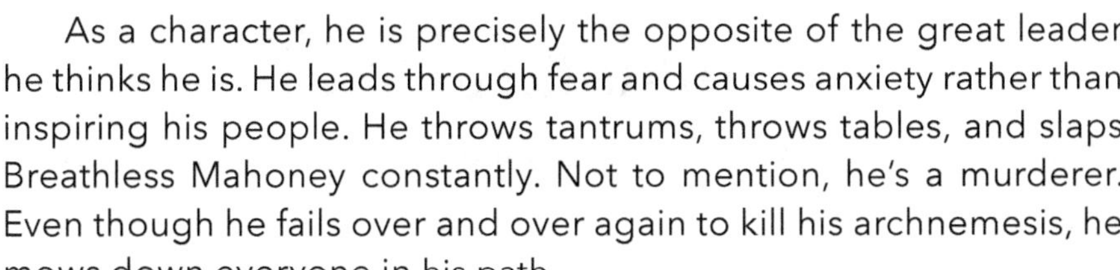

As a character, he is precisely the opposite of the great leader he thinks he is. He leads through fear and causes anxiety rather than inspiring his people. He throws tantrums, throws tables, and slaps Breathless Mahoney constantly. Not to mention, he's a murderer. Even though he fails over and over again to kill his archnemesis, he mows down everyone in his path.

That is not the kind of leader I want to be. I want to inspire the best in people, not continually drag out the worst. I want to build them up, not tear them down or murder them. I want to flip a table over in collective triumph, not while screaming in anger. A good team needs generals and foot soldiers because everyone can bring value in their own way.

Keep Big Boy on the screen. Keep him out of the project space.

Dragonheart (1996)

Starring Dennis Quaid, Sean Connery (voice), David Thewlis

The Quote

BOWEN: *You said the words! You spoke them from your heart!*

KING EINON: *I vomited them up because I couldn't stomach them! Because I knew it was what you wanted to hear!*

The Context

Bowen is a knight with a pure heart. When Einon was a boy, Bowen trained him to be a knight, imbued with valor and virtue, defending the weak and the truth, and undoing wickedness. Einon was injured, and his heart was replaced with part of one from a dragon. As King Einon grew up, he became a cruel dictator and acted in opposition to the creed he was taught.

Bowen assumed that the dragon's heart had corrupted Einon. Upon confronting him, Einon admits that he did not believe in Bowen's teachings from the start. He only told Bowen what he wanted to hear.

The Lesson

True believers are hard to find.

When I watched this movie for the first time, I was genuinely heartbroken for Bowen. The reveal that none of Bowen's teachings took hold in Einon's soul temporarily broke him. As the old saying goes, "You can lead a horse to water, but you can't make it drink."

Hope is a vital feeling to hold onto–to believe that the best in people will emerge. Too many people to count have let me down. Yet I still assume the best when I meet someone new. From successful first dates that go nowhere to presidential elections that defy the projections, we've all been told one thing and then something else happens.

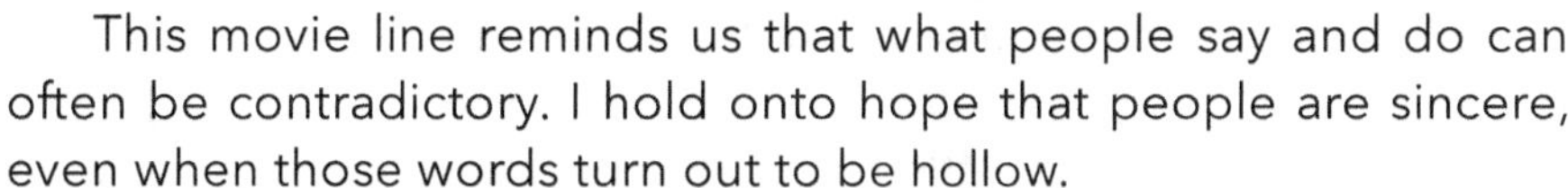

This movie line reminds us that what people say and do can often be contradictory. I hold onto hope that people are sincere, even when those words turn out to be hollow.

Face/Off (1997)

Starring John Travolta, Nicholas Cage

The Quote

CASTOR TROY: *Isn't this religious? Ah yes. The eternal battle between good and evil, saint and sinners … but you're still not having any FUN!*

The Context

Obsessed with bringing a terrorist to justice, FBI Agent Sean Archer has been chasing Castor Troy everywhere, trading everything from bullets to faces. In their final face off, they end up in a church, ready to try once more to rid the world of each other. As always, Castor is ready to have some fun!

The Lesson

No matter the stakes, the situation, the enemy, or the battle, there is always time to have some fun!

I remember one time when I was producing my practicum film *Pirates and Pills* at Columbia College Chicago. The crew had already spent several days together on location, and we had several more to look forward to on the stage where we built three-quarters of a pirate ship deck.

On this particular day, we were filming at a residential house in the suburbs in the backyard. We took a break, and I walked out the front door to see the camera, lighting, and grip crew doing what became known as "Grip Olympics." From what I could remember, they were doing lighting stand lifts, the sandbag tosses, apple-box jumps, and grip yoga. They were having a blast bonding, enduring the sometimes boring set life, and staying healthy.

It was at that moment that I realized that as long as the job was getting done, you could have fun on a film set. And if the job isn't getting done, maybe a little fun is needed to inspire the crew to act. Fun and food are what keep a set going. That day, I bought a box of cookies as a surprise to counteract all of the calories they burned in the Grip Olympics, and it was the best investment of the entire shoot.

From that moment on, when I face off against good and evil, I look to the most serious person in the room and remind them that "they are still not having any fun," in hopes they will smile.

Fight Club (1999)

Starring Edward Norton, Brad Pitt

The Quote

TYLER DURDEN: *Hitting bottom isn't a weekend retreat. It's not a goddamn seminar. Stop trying to control everything and just let go! LET GO!*

The Context

A depressed man suffering from insomnia meets a strange soap salesman named Tyler Durden and soon finds himself living in his squalid house after his perfect apartment is destroyed. The two bored men form an underground club with strict rules and fight other men who are fed up with their mundane lives.

The Lesson

Not trying to control everything—letting go—has become my life philosophy, but it has been the hardest lesson to practice. For too long, I thought that if I could just make things happen, they would happen. I could do anything as long as I put my mind to it. Try, try again.

What followed were years of playing chess with people and situations. I needed something to happen, so I had to find this person, make that happen, and then get this other person to talk to the other person ... on and on, spinning plates in the hope that all that kinetic energy would light the bulb of the original idea.

One day, when I lived in San Francisco, I was driving all over the Bay area, threading the needle, working for three different film festivals at the same time. I was running so much that day that I ran out of gas–literally and figuratively. I had just enough gasoline to get off the highway and crawl to a stop on a hilly forestry road.

While waiting for assistance to arrive, I realized I was stressed, tired, and unfulfilled. I hit rock bottom. I needed to make a big change. I wrote a letter of resignation to myself, stating I was done trying to control everything and be everything to everyone. It started me on a path of focusing on one job at a time and on myself. I had to let go of everything that wasn't important or that wouldn't bring me joy.

I'm not an advocate for taking extreme actions like those taken in this movie. But I am an advocate for whatever action these words embody for you. No motivational video, poster, or book can tell YOU how to live YOUR life. Improvement is a choice, and it begins with relinquishing control over what you cannot control. In other words, "Stop trying to control everything and just let go! LET GO!"

Friends (1994-2004)

Season 9, Episode 7

Starring Jennifer Aniston, Courteney Cox, Lisa Kudrow, Matt LeBlanc, Matthew Perry, David Schwimmer

The Quote

CHANDLER: *Get there faster!*

The Context

Chandler and Joey find a video tape with Monica's name on it in her ex-boyfriend's apartment. Chandler and the audience immediately realize that it could be a tape of an intimate encounter between Monica and her ex. Joey is slowly catching up. Almost there. Nearly got it. After an almost uncomfortable amount of time, Chandler yells, "Get there faster!" and Joey immediately gets the point.

The Lesson

We all know that person. The friend who takes a loooooong time telling a story. The coworker who makes extra time to come to a conclusion you came to minutes ago. As a parent I have had my share of moments watching my child flying round and round the point while I sit patiently waiting for them to land the plane.

Friends was great about making the smallest moments of our existence visible and funny. Though I have never used this line out loud, I am constantly screaming it in my own head while outwardly showing the patience social decorum demands.

Throughout my life I have learned acceptance. We all learn, live, talk, think, and listen in different ways and at different speeds. It is important to accept people as they are and find common ground. It is also important to accept that we, too, are only human, and that impatience is par for the course. A little interior humor can go a long way toward making it through life with the other humans we encounter.

The Fugitive (1993)

Starring Harrison Ford, Tommy Lee Jones

The Quote

DR. RICHARD KIMBLE: *Well, I am trying to solve a puzzle. And I just found a big piece!*

The Context

Dr. Kimble is a fugitive, falsely accused of killing his wife. Deputy Sam Gerrard is on a mission to capture him using all means at his disposal. Gerrard's goal is simple, but it is made increasingly complicated as Kimble continues to solve each one of his goals: escape, survive, escape again, survive, find out who killed his wife, escape again, find the man who killed her, survive, find who hired that man, survive, confront, escape, survive, prove his innocence.

Every time the two of them speak, Kimble repeats his innocence, and Gerrard states his sole intention is to catch Kimble. Kimble's innocence is inconsequential to Gerrard. And when Kimble learns the truth, he is ahead of his captors and conspirators for the first time and states, "Well, I am trying to solve a puzzle. And I just found a big piece!"

The Lesson

Solve your own puzzle.

We all have different goals to accomplish. Some of us have the empathy needed to see another person's struggle. Others blindly follow their own path, oblivious to how it may hurt another person's journey. Gerrard wasn't wrong in focusing on his singular goal, but he didn't realize until much later in the chase that he was making Kimble's journey even harder, that he was actually innocent. He remains skeptical until the very end, even though the clues in Kimble's favor were stacking up, which is why we feel the joy in Kimble's voice when he finally catches a break.

Our life puzzle is our own to build. No friend or family member can know exactly what it is like to be us. We are not alone, but only we can truly know the significance of finding and shaping each piece of our puzzle.

Every job we do, person we experience, step we take, and moment we breathe can hold a clue to the reason we exist. Each moment brings us closer to knowing what we become. Like Dr. Kimble, we should take a moment to enjoy the puzzle pieces we find, even though the Gerrards in our lives don't truly understand what it means to us. Either they will eventually understand, or they will give up and move on to the next fugitive.

The General's Daughter (1999)

Starring John Travolta, Madeleine Stowe, James Cromwell

The Quote

BRENNER: *Oh, unclench your ass cheeks, Dalbert. The scary part is over.*

The Context

Agent Brenner is undercover, armed with nothing but his wits and a cheesy southern accent. When things get tense with his target, his accomplice, Dalbert, gets scared. After the target calms down, Brenner drops this hilarious line to ease the tension even more.

The Lesson

Defuse the tension with truthful humor. Many times I have used the unvarnished truth to help calm the moment. I worked in my college film program for three years. In the first two years, I handled every insane idea, debate, and emergency thrown my way. In my third year, I became worn out from dealing with everyone's problems.

I sometimes diffused my own tension when hearing an insane problem by saying, "I hate you all!" Everyone would constantly laugh at my exhaustion, thinking it was a joke. It would defuse the tension and help us move forward. The funny part is that sometimes I was serious about it. But no one could tell when I was serious or joking. I was able to mask the truth with humor and move on.

Since then, I have used variations of "unclench your ass cheeks," and it has always encouraged people to calm down. Quite the opposite happens when you tell people to calm down; they usually get more intense or stressed. You can best help the Dalberts of the world get through the scary parts by making them laugh.

Heat (1995)

Starring Al Pacino, Robert De Niro, Val Kilmer, Jon Voight

The Quote

VINCENT HANNA: *I gotta hold on to my angst. I preserve it because I need it. It keeps me sharp, on the edge, where I gotta be.*

The Context

Vincent Hanna is the head of an elite police task force that takes down the toughest robbery-homicide crews. He is highly dedicated, to the detriment of his marriages. His current wife describes him as a prowling hunter who surveys the terrain and does not stop until he runs down his prey. He also doesn't share himself and his life with her, as she only gets the leftovers.

He replies, "I gotta hold on to my angst. I preserve it because I need it. It keeps me sharp, on the edge, where I gotta be."

The Lesson

Had I written this book over fifteen years ago, The Lesson would have been to hold it all in and use it to keep going. I lived a life full of angst, and my personal and professional lives weren't where I wanted them to be. I would use that fuel to be in two places at once, to solve multiple problems at the same time, and to be everything to everyone I knew.

Since then, I have learned that holding all of that pain and anger inside can be self-destructive. The worst part is that when you hide your pain, no one knows you're suffering. They either can't help you or they unknowingly pile on, making it infinitely worse. Having an outlet for your angst is an excellent way of dealing with it. Whether it be a physical outlet such as boxing or dancing, a mental one such as meditation or writing, or an interpersonal one such as talking to a friend or therapist, it helps to let go of that angst and focus on what is really important to you.

I am an advocate of balance. There are times to use those emotions to push yourself further and times to release them to avoid burnout. This quote serves both purposes. When I need to shift into a new gear, it pops into my head. I ask myself, "Do I really need to hold on to this angst? Do I really need to use it? Or am I being dramatic and about to hit an emotional brick wall?" In that moment, the quote reminds me to relax.

The Quote

VINCENT HANNA: *Back to work.*

The Context

Hanna and his fellow officers are close to catching a group of expert thieves in the act of robbing a warehouse. Hidden in box trucks, the officers observe them. Most of the officers are patient, but one paces back and forth. When he finally takes a seat, his weapon bangs against the truck, which alerts the bad guys, causing them to abort the plan without having stolen anything.

After the area is clear, the cops emerge. Hanna stares down the officer who just spoiled hours and hours of work setting up the trap. As morning approaches, he wearily remarks, "Back to work" and walks away.

The Lesson

Setbacks happen. Keep going.

There's always that one person who screws up and makes more work for everyone else. When that happens, remind yourself that they probably didn't do it on purpose, and accept that more work is needed to complete the project. It is what it is. Let them off the hook (and maybe off the project) and promptly go "back to work."

Hook (1991)

Starring Robin Williams, Dustin Hoffman, Julia Roberts

The Quote

CAPTAIN HOOK: *Are you ready for me, Peter? Come on, humor the Hook.*

The Context

Peter Pan is about to face off with Captain James Hook for the last time. Hook has the war he's been dreaming of. Pan wants this conflict to end. Hook taunts him, "Are you ready for me, Peter? Come on, humor the Hook."

The Lesson

Face your problems like a villain.

While I do not live in a fantasy world called Neverland, I do live in a world with challenges. And when I face those challenges, I look them in the figurative eye and say, "Come on, humor the Hook." I want my future self to be proud of the problems my present self has bested. It is like a dance I'll never shy away from—an exciting adventure to shake away the boredom.

I don't go looking for problems (anymore). But when they appear, it helps to up the drama (in my mind) and prepare to fence with them all the while knowing that I will find a solution. While villains are evil, the great ones have a lot of fun while villainizing. Be the villain of the problems in your life.

The Quote

PETER: *Jack, you won't believe this: I found my happy thought. It took me three days, then guess what happened when I did? Up I went! You know what my happy thought was? It was you.*

The Context

Peter Pan grew up and forgot everything about his life of swashbuckling adventures fighting against Captain Hook in Neverland. When his children are kidnapped, he must embark on a journey to remember how to do all the things he used to, including how to fly. To fly, you must find your happy thought and hold onto it. After days of failing, Pan finally finds his happy thought while thinking of the moment his son was born.

The Lesson

Find your happy thought and hold it close.

During the pandemic, I experienced the lowest emotional point in my life. I didn't think I was useful or had done anything good in my life. Since I tied my self-worth to how useful I was, I felt worthless. I came across an old photo that reminded me of something I had done to make another person's life better. Then another. Since I keep everything, it was easy to find digital moments that helped me feel better.

I decided to collect every digital memento I could find that proved I had worth. I started with pictures of important moments. Then I moved on to news articles in which I was quoted, key production documents that led to a victorious project, and screenshots of thank-you notes. Lastly, I collected all the video projects I had worked on. I placed all of these things on a flash drive. I call it my "Happy Thoughts" drive. It is like a time capsule, but I carry it around with me and continue to add memories to it.

Whenever I feel like I'm not doing enough in my life, I look at the drive and remind myself that I have done enough. Once in a while, I plug it in and randomly pull up a moment and ruminate on the people I worked with and the good we accomplished. Obviously, there are many memories of my son. The moment I met him. The moments that mattered. The moments that made me proud to be a dad, a role I never thought I would be able to play.

One day, when I am gone, I hope my son will pull out that drive and, like the pensive in Harry Potter, can take my "tears", access my memories, and see the good I accomplished and know how every moment of my life was meant to make him better. Until that

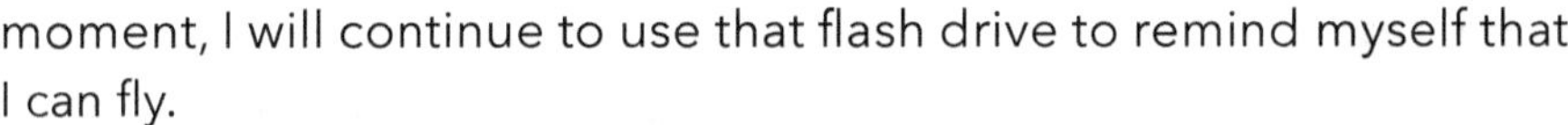

moment, I will continue to use that flash drive to remind myself that I can fly.

The Quote

PETER BANNING: *To live ... to live would be an awfully big adventure.*

The Context

Peter Pan has remembered what it's like to live.

The Lesson

I use this quote to remind myself to live as fully as I can. Every minute can't be an adventure. There can be boring times waiting for the next step of the adventure, but I remind myself to participate fully in life every chance I get.

Years ago, I had one "day of jubilee" (from Toby Ziegler, *The West Wing*) every year. Then I started to realize how short life was and that my whole life can be filled with jubilee, at any point. All I have to do is step up to the adventure that awaits.

The Insider (1999)

Starring Al Pacino, Russell Crowe, Christopher Plummer

The Quotes

LOWELL BERGMAN: *And Jeffrey Wigand, who's out on a limb, does he go on television and tell the truth? Yes. Is it newsworthy? Yes. Are we gonna air it? Of course not. Why? Because he's not telling the truth? No. Because he IS telling the truth. That's why we're not going to air it. And the more truth he tells, the worse it gets!*

LOWELL BERGMAN: *Obey orders and fuck off. That's what I hear.*

The Context

Lowell is the producer of the investigative news show *60 Minutes*. His job involves finding and securing interview candidates for his host and partner, Mike Wallace. The job is challenging because sometimes sources talk when they shouldn't, as is the case with Jeffrey Wigand, a former corporate officer with a major tobacco company. Big Tobacco has deep pockets and threatens Wigand in every way to prevent him from revealing the truth about their product. This includes threatening the company that owns *60 Minutes*. Lowell's professional integrity is at stake as he fights to get his show on the air despite mounting pressure from all sides.

The Lesson

Ask yourself, what kind of person would you like to be? Because one day, you will be put to the test.

Lowell is the kind of producer I have always aspired to be. First off, he is a great storyteller. Not only are his investigative stories well laid out, but he can also tell the real-life story of the current situation in a succinct way. The first quote exposes the hypocrisy of the network, showing that everything Jeffrey said is true, but they won't air his story because "the more truth he tells, the worse it gets!"

Lowell is also incredibly direct and to the point, as shown in the second quote. Instead of beating around the bush and accepting the false veneer he's been given, he reads between the lines and points out that they are being told to "obey orders and fuck off." I have been in too many situations where something just didn't feel right, yet the staff are told to do it anyway. I pride myself on bringing honest truth to every professional conversation, whether it's with the janitor or the chairman of the board.

Additionally, Lowell is a man of his word. When you start a job that requires a high level of trust, you have to adhere to that standard at all times. Lowell made an early decision that nothing would compromise his integrity. Only he can control how far he's willing to go to get the story. But he says he never left a source out to dry. And I, too, never want to betray a cast or crew member.

When that trust is broken, it rarely gets restored. Lowell also refers to the broken trust between him and his partner, Mike, who

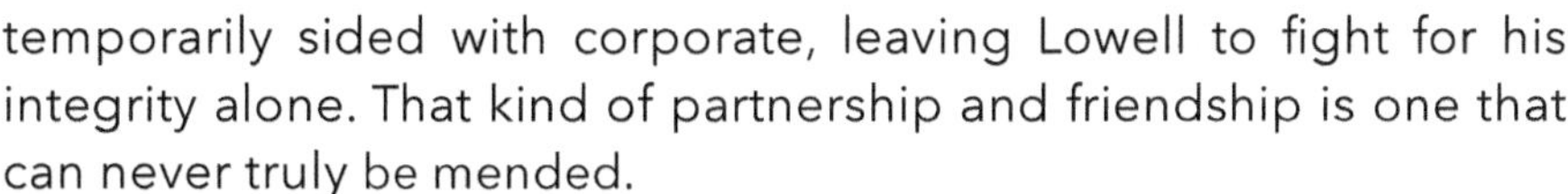

temporarily sided with corporate, leaving Lowell to fight for his integrity alone. That kind of partnership and friendship is one that can never truly be mended.

What is your integrity, your work ethic, and your word worth? Times may come when you are pressured in ways you never imagined. Only you can determine your breaking point and what you're willing to endure for what you believe. Know yourself.

The Quote

LOWELL BERGMAN: *If they can catch you in a lie, they can paint everything with that brush.*

The Context

Lowell has been defending Jeffrey because Jeffrey is the victim of a smear campaign designed to discredit him before his damning testimony is revealed to the court of public opinion. The problem is that some points in the smear campaign are somewhat true but need more context. Jeffrey believes these things are irrelevant to his testimony. Lowell tries in vain to make Jeffrey realize that if he is caught in a lie, then they can "use that brush" to paint everything Jeffrey says as false, including his testimony.

The Lesson

You cannot paint everything with the same brush.

I often use this quote when discussing politics. People tend to categorize and assume that everything fitting a category is the same. "All Black people do this ..." "Many women do that ..." "Everyone at this company believes ..." Such generalizations are dangerous and can distract from the truth. People are complex. Situations are even more complex. No two people or situations are exactly alike.

Imagine a house being painted. No wall is exactly the same or made of the same material, and none can be painted exactly the same way. Some walls need more coats of paint than others. Some are more exposed to the sun and require different treatment. Every wall has countless tiny imperfections, making no two walls identical. The idea of using a single brush to paint an entire house the same way is a myth. Different brushes and paints are needed to cover all surfaces.

We are also incredibly complex and nuanced. In Jeffrey's case, the lawsuit he faced was over a cheap can opener that didn't work, and he refused to pay for it. That has little to do with his testimony on the deadly effects of tobacco. Remember, context matters.

The Jackal (1997)

Starring Bruce Willis, Richard Gere, Sidney Poitier

The Quote

CARTER PRESTON: *Witherspoon, you by-the-book asshole.*

The Context

Agent Witherspoon is an FBI agent who works with Deputy Director Carter Preston and convict Declan Mulqueen as they hunt for the infamous killer known as The Jackal. Agent Preston's team has found a lead, and Preston orders them not to include this information in the official report. Along the way, they discover a mole within their team.

Further investigation reveals that Agent Witherspoon went against protocol by including the information in the report, which The Jackal now has. This action endangers several lives, including Witherspoon's, and Preston is furious!

The Lesson

Learn to step away from "the book."

Proper procedures exist to maintain order and efficiency in any situation. Whether you're building a car, babysitting children, or hunting an international fugitive, rules help ensure the job gets done and everyone stays safe.

However, blindly following procedures can lead to disaster. It's crucial to understand why these rules are in place and to trust your judgment and your team's when circumstances change. It's impossible to create a rule or procedure for every situation. Unexpected scenarios will always occur that aren't covered in the manual. It takes skill and experience to know when to think outside the box and find new ways to complete the task.

Strictly sticking to "the book" should never be an excuse. When disaster hits, that book will still be there, taking up space.

Jurassic Park (1993)

Starring Sam Neill, Laura Dern, Jeff Goldblum

The Quote

DR. IAN MALCOLM: *Yeah, yeah, but your scientists were so preoccupied with whether or not they could that they didn't stop to think if they should.*

The Context

John Hammond has found a way to bring dinosaurs back to life! His scientists made a groundbreaking discovery and now have an island full of the creatures. Due to an accident, Hammond is forced to bring in a group of experts to explore the island. To Hammond's surprise, a cushy dinner turns into a vigorous debate over the consequences of taking such an ill-conceived action.

The Lesson

We can do anything, but we should not do everything. Some plans belong in the idea stage.

Our history is littered with technological, biological, sociological, and psychological advancements. We study, we test, we create, we repeat. As a race, we are natural-born innovators. One thing we are not great at is questioning those innovations. Why are we making the thing we have discovered? What are the consequences? Are all voices considered when implementing this new thing? We are so excited by our own intellect and the increasing pace of our discoveries that we sometimes create the thing that will destroy us.

I love it when people are excited.

But when a business becomes excited about "the next new thing," like cryptocurrency, AI, or laser discs, they put everything into it. It is the only thing that everyone should be buying into right now. It is a fad. And Wikipedia is full of articles about fads that failed after millions pledged allegiance to them.

In the late 1990s, tech retailer Circuit City created a rentable DVD system called DIVX. Every time I went to Circuit City, I saw the advertisements next to the same looped clip of the tornado taking Jo's truck in the movie *Twister*. The gimmick was that you bought a DVD that was playable for two days, but if you needed more than forty-eight hours to watch the movie, you could pay to get extra time to watch it. It was the new thing, and "everyone" was on board. It died within two years. I doubt anyone in those early development meetings asked whether they should create this new system.

Innovation is a key part of our survival. But rushed innovation or blind acceptance of an innovation has the potential to damage our survival. Life is fragile, so we should be extra careful with what innovations we allow to exist. If we actually found a way to recreate dinosaurs, there would be no guarantee they would not be as vicious or violent as they are depicted in this movie. Nevertheless, it's likely that tech developers wouldn't hesitate to activate them even faster in real life.

Liar Liar (1997)

Starring Jim Carrey, Maura Tierney, Justin Cooper

The Quote

JUDGE MARSHALL STEVENS: *It is only out of sheer morbid curiosity that I am allowing this freak show to continue.*

The Context

Fletcher Reede is having a rough day. He is a lawyer who can't tell a lie, which conflicts with his usual approach and natural instincts. The judge overseeing his current case watches in horror as Fletcher's unpredictable behavior worsens. Suddenly, Fletcher realizes that the truth might actually help him. The judge has reached his limit with Fletcher's manic antics, but curiosity wins out, and he allows Fletcher to present his final argument.

The Lesson

I often use this line. Sometimes chaos feels very close. We can choose to shut everything down and walk away. But what if we let the chaos continue? Maybe this is the moment when inspiration is born. Maybe the house will come crashing down. One thing is certain: Craziness keeps boredom at bay.

When someone asks, "Do you want to know what ridiculous thing just happened?" I reply, "Only out of sheer morbid curiosity." We love to watch a train wreck. It's why we cover our eyes during scary movies but peek through our fingers. It's why we yell at the TV when we watch the news. Our curiosity drives us into uncomfortable places, which can lead to discoveries or simply jolt us out of apathy. It can also be fun, making a quiet moment a bit more dramatic.

"Out of sheer morbid curiosity" has become my go-to phrase when facing the unexpected.

The Lost World: Jurassic Park (1997)

Starring Jeff Goldblum, Julianne Moore, Arliss Howard

The Quote

DR. IAN MALCOLM: *Taking dinosaurs off this island is the worst idea in the long, sad history of bad ideas. And, uh, I'm gonna be there when you learn that.*

The Context

In the first *Jurassic Park*, Ian Malcolm was the suave jokester of the group. Whenever he wasn't sleazy, he was making excellent points about the "rape of the natural world." After surviving the deadly events of the first movie, he was unwittingly forced into returning to the land of the dinosaurs.

What lacks in humor this time around he makes up for in trying his best to warn everyone about how much of a bad idea this is. Obviously, no one listens, but he is proven right every step of the way. Putting people with dinosaurs is a bad idea.

The Lesson

I am a huge fan of collaboration. All points are valid. No idea is a bad idea. Everyone has a voice. We are all in this together.

But sometimes, we need to be honest with ourselves and each other and just call it like it is. Sometimes, an idea can be so monumentally bad that it never should have been considered in the first place. What I love about these lines from Dr. Malcolm is that he clearly states that.

I loved watching him be right.

The Matrix (1999)

Starring Keanu Reeves, Laurence Fishburne, Carrie-Anne Moss

The Quote

MORPHEUS: *This is your last chance. After this, there is no turning back. You take the blue pill, the story ends. You wake up in your bed, and believe whatever you want to believe. You take the red pill, you stay in Wonderland, and I show you how deep the rabbit hole goes.*

The Context

Neo has been living in a world he believed was real. He heard stories about a mysterious man named Morpheus. One day, Morpheus initiates the events that lead to their meeting. Morpheus reveals that this is not the real world and that Neo must now make a choice. Take the blue pill and stay in the fake world, or take the red pill and learn the truth, potentially changing his life forever.

The Lesson

On my nineteenth birthday–September 6, 2001–I was working at Columbia College Chicago's art galleries, newly obsessed with Alicia Key's "Caged Bird." My parents had divorced years earlier after a public blowup in an Indiana grocery store, and I had sided with my father, having absorbed his resentment and rigid worldview. Despite my loyalty, his anger often redirected itself toward me. That night, after our usual grocery trip to Indiana, we sat in the car eating White Castle when he raised a topic he rarely touched with compassion: my mother. Instead of berating her, he demanded–aggressively–that I forgive her. When I said I needed time, he snapped that I was unfit for God because I couldn't forgive instantly. Something in me broke.

I went silent on the car ride home–an unforgivable act in his eyes. But I didn't care. Back home, he waited for me to speak, seething. Instead, I quietly packed two bags, said goodbye, and walked out into the midnight rain. I had no money and no plan, just Alicia Keys in my head: "Right now, I feel like a bird / Caged without a key." I wandered until I caught a bus, eventually ending up at my best friend Chris's place, where he and others helped me gather essentials. For the first time, I felt the possibility of living a life that belonged to me.

Five days later, on the morning of September 11, I rewatched *The Matrix*. When Neo faced the red-pill/blue-pill choice, time seemed to slow. I realized I was facing the same decision: go back to the familiar pain I'd fled, or venture into a terrifying, undefined future. I chose the red pill–consciously, deliberately. Moments later, Chris burst from his room: a plane had hit the World Trade Center. The world was suddenly changed, as if my choice had opened the door to chaos.

That night, shaken by the attacks, I called my father. He told me to come home, and I did, but when he treated my departure as a temporary rebellion and assumed I'd stay, I recognized the truth: Leaving wasn't a punishment he chose for me; it was a choice I had to make for myself. For the first time, I told him no and walked back out into my life. I've never doubted that decision. It's moments like that–cinematic, symbolic, and deeply human–that shape us and reveal who we are, and that's why I wrote this book.

The Negotiator (1998)

Starring Samuel L. Jackson, Kevin Spacey, David Morse

The Quote

LT. CHRIS SABIAN: *I can't believe this. I'm just surrounded by a room of people who wanna go in there and kill him. This is the guy who calls you a friend. I got nothing invested in this. I wonder why that is, or maybe someday we'll find out.*

The Context

Danny Roman is a cop and negotiator falsely accused of killing another officer. Trapped and now a hostage taker, he buys time while desperately searching for the real killer. He finds it hard to trust his friends. In his own words, "When your friends betray you, sometimes the only people you can trust are strangers." Enter Chris Sabian, another negotiator with no prior ties to anyone involved in the standoff. He gradually realizes that he can't trust anyone and that everyone is against him.

The Lesson

As a producer, I'm constantly stepping into situations where everyone involved has already chosen sides. It might be something small, like the color of a mug in the shot, or something larger, like whether the project should even exist. In these tense moments, it's crucial to stay calm and listen to both sides.

Find a way to let everyone feel heard, then negotiate a solution that allows each person to get some of what they want. If the issue is black-and-white, help each side reach what you see as the best choice to maintain collaboration.

Try not to get caught up in the argument, as passionate people can sometimes see even the most minor disagreements, like the mug color, as life or death. All they need is a reminder of why everyone is there and that there's a lot to gain beyond this current negotiation.

The Quote

DANNY ROMAN: *You can't talk me down! You can't make me change the deadline! Now get me Sabian! You've got six minutes! 42, 41, 40 ...*

The Context

Danny has just taken hostages and asked for Chris Sabian, the negotiator. Chris is in another part of town and won't make it by Danny's deadline. Another officer tries to negotiate but fails every one of Danny's tests. Showing how serious he is, Danny screams into the walkie-talkie and gives a clear countdown.

The Lesson

Manage expectations in the clearest way.

As a producer I've learned how beneficial clear and direct communication is. Does it work or doesn't it? What do we need to make it work? How much will it cost? How much time do we have? While filmmaking isn't life or death like surgery (for example), there is a lot at stake—money, time, people's livelihoods, and their dreams of creating something great.

One miscommunication can cause a prop to be measured wrong, a day to go over schedule and budget, the wrong person to be hired, or a stunt to go wrong, causing injury or death. Often, miscommunication can mess up lunch, leading to an angry crew.

I do my best to communicate and overcommunicate what's expected of each person and how long things will take, and I ensure everyone has the current, relevant information. If I tell you we have thirty-five minutes to shoot this scene, we have thirty-five minutes. I might have an extra twenty minutes tucked away, but only because I know people are human and we might go over. If we're twenty minutes late, we're still on schedule.

The same applies to production. While I don't condone yelling, clearly communicating that we have (as character Danny Roman would say) "six minutes, forty-two, forty-one" (or however you wish to count down before lunch or any event) helps the crew understand what's at stake and prepare for the next phase together. When lunch is involved, everyone listens closely.

The Peacemaker (1997)

Starring George Clooney, Nicole Kidman

The Quote

JULIA KELLY: *I'm not afraid of the man who wants ten nuclear weapons, Colonel. I'm terrified of the man who only wants one.*

The Context

National Security Council official Julia Kelly and military intelligence Lieutenant Colonel Tom Devoe are investigating the theft of nuclear warheads from Russia by an unknown enemy. Tom thinks he is a typical terrorist, but Julia looks deeper into the suspect's profile and explains that there are other motivations besides money, power, and terror.

The Lesson

Motivations matter.

Movies often make us believe that villains are simply evil individuals with twirling mustaches who are ready to cause harm because that's what bad guys do.

However, no one is that straightforward. This movie was among the first to portray villains being as nuanced and complex as the heroes we follow. Everyone has deeper reasons for their actions than merely being good or bad. There is a purpose behind everything, and we are all the hero or heroine in our own story. We justify our actions regardless of the circumstances.

Before watching this movie, I would have thought that the only reason someone would want nuclear warheads would be to maintain or obtain power. Any generic mustache-twirling villain would do; this person is just evil. It was only after the thought exercise this movie inspired that I realized that the person wanting one will most likely want to use it and have their own justified reason for doing so.

I carry that lesson into my daily life. The office bureaucrat who implements processes that make others' lives difficult is not doing so out of malice but because they believe these actions serve the company's best interests. Right or wrong, they feel they are doing the right thing. Before opposing those practices (as I genuinely believe we should protect the people and the company), I try to understand why they were put in place and the motivation of the person who initiated these actions.

Understanding their motivations allows me to empathize with those in power and provides a way to voice the suffering of the people. This enables me to advocate for solutions that help employees while also addressing the problems the original measures were designed to solve.

Look at all sides of the problem and try to understand the motivations of everyone involved, as there might be someone in a volatile situation who wants only one metaphorical warhead.

Reservoir Dogs (1992)

Starring Harvey Keitel, Tim Roth, Michael Madsen, Steve Buscemi

The Quote

MR. WHITE: *For the past fifteen minutes, you've been droning on about names. Toby. Toby? Toby? Toby Wong. Toby Wong? Toby Wong. Toby Chung? Fucking Charlie Chan. I got Madonna's big dick coming out of my left ear, and Toby the Jap … I don't know what, comin' out of my right.*

The Context

A group of men sits at a diner finishing their breakfast. Mr. Pink is telling a story about the origin of the song "Like a Virgin" by Madonna. Joe is flipping through his address book, trying to remember someone named Toby. Between them is Mr. White, who has had enough of their droning. He takes Joe's book and goes off on the group, mocking Joe's repetition.

The Lesson

Human interaction can be chaotic. But sometimes that chaos can be precisely what you need to grow.

I am a patient person, but am so only out of a lack of options. Sometimes you have no option but to wait for the next show to drop or a piece of the puzzle to fit. But if it were all up to me, I would have every answer I was seeking now. Does she like me? Did I get the job? What will happen next season?

I do have impatience with people. I am Mr. White. Sometimes people can talk on and on and on about a topic that no one else in the room cares about. My lighthearted internal disdain for over-talkers stems from experience with my father. For years, he would talk to me about whatever interested him. From music to people he didn't like, he would go on and on about what he thought was right or wrong. And he was 100 percent right and everyone else was wrong. Such is the human ego. But as I grew older, I began to realize what he thought was a conversation was actually a sermon. He would not let the other person talk, and when they did, he would quickly steer control of the thought back to himself.

In the years after I moved out on my own, I would come back a few times a year to help him with tasks he didn't want to handle. I would inevitably get drawn into a "conversation" with him. One time, he went eleven minutes talking nonstop, only to pause for my complete agreement before continuing.

Today, I have many people in my life, and some of them trigger my impatience when they talk nonstop. I even have that person who will try to remember something, but repeats a keyword over and over and over again. Sometimes I say to them, "Toby? Toby. Toby? Toby." They never get it. But it reminds me that even though I am annoyed, I can have fun from the moment, and maybe I just need to ride out the "Toby" line of thought. It is possible that their droning can lead to an important discovery. Maybe Toby is someone I should also know.

Robin Hood: Prince of Thieves (1991)

Starring Kevin Costner, Morgan Freeman, Alan Rickman

The Quote

SHERIFF OF NOTTINGHAM: *Locksley, I'll cut your heart out with a spoon*

ROBIN HOOD: *Then it begins.*

GUY OF GISBORNE: *Why a spoon, cousin? Why not an axe?*

SHERIFF OF NOTTINGHAM: *Because it's DULL, you twit. It'll hurt more.*

SHERIFF OF NOTTINGHAM (AFTER HE STABS SIR GUY OF GISBORNE): *At least I didn't use a spoon.*

The Context

At first, Robin (Locksley) Hood was a nuisance to the evil Sheriff of Nottingham. Now they have come face-to-face for the first time. Both in shock, Robin strikes first and wounds the Sheriff's pride ... and his face. Robin mounts a sudden and daring escape. The Sheriff, reeling, shouts, "Locksley, I'll cut your heart out with a spoon." Thus begins their battle and our obsession with the spoon.

Later, Guy of Gisborne, the Sheriff's cousin, questions why he would use a spoon in his threat. Later on, when Guy has failed once more to capture Robin Hood, the Sheriff kills him and launches one last taunt.

The Lesson

If you are going to threaten someone, make it memorable!

The Rock (1996)

Starring Sean Connery, Nicolas Cage, Ed Harris

The Quote

COMMANDER ANDERSON: *I cannot give that order! I will not give that order!*

The Context

A team of mercenaries, led by General Hummel, has taken hostages on Alcatraz Island in order to avenge fellow Marines whom they feel the government has used and discarded. A team of Marines, led by Commander Anderson, is sent in to save the day. They successfully infiltrate the island but are outmaneuvered and surrounded by the mercenaries.

In a tense standoff, Anderson tries to explain to Hummel that this is not the way to get justice. Hummel repeatedly orders Anderson to surrender, and Anderson refuses every time. It becomes clear that although Hummel has his reasons for taking this action, he is bluffing and really doesn't want to take any lives.

The Lesson

Even if you lose, at least you stay true to yourself.

I admired Anderson for standing his ground. Before this moment, the Marines hold a mission briefing and load onto a helicopter in the most heroic display of force ever. I wanted to be these guys. They are on a mission to save lives. But then they are cornered in the first third of the movie. How could this happen?

Heroes can fail. They can get cornered, captured, or lose the moment. But they are still heroes. When they are exposed, Anderson stands tall, makes his case, and stays firm. He could have surrendered and possibly saved his men's lives. They might have had a chance to break free after surrendering and overtake the mercenaries. We will never know.

I appreciated his honesty and bravery in the face of death. Sometimes giving up cannot be negotiated. Having a clear understanding of your purpose and your mission, and ensuring everyone understands it, is the only way to win.

Ronin (1998)

Starring Robert De Niro, Jean Reno, Natascha McElhone

The Quotes

SAM: *Either you're part of the problem or you're part of the solution, or you're just part of the landscape.*

SAM: *Tell me about an ambush? Tell me about an ambush? I ambushed you with a cup of coffee!*

The Context

Sam is an ex-spy turned freelancer who has been tasked with stealing a mysterious package. He is brought together with like-minded individuals whose identities are as mysterious as their target. One member of the team, Spence, immediately establishes dominance with his superior skill set.

Sam begins to realize that Spence might talk a good game, but he has sloppy follow-through. While Spence outlines a possible strategy for ambushing the owners of the case, Sam casually puts his coffee cup on a nearby table. He then confronts Spence with the foolishness of his own plan. When Spence takes offense to being challenged, Sam questions the legitimacy of Spence's background while forcing him to back into the coffee cup. Distracted by the coffee, Sam seizes the moment, takes Spence's gun, and restrains him.

As the group watches, Sam states, "Tell me about an ambush? Tell me about an ambush? I ambushed you with a cup of coffee!" proving Spence's incompetence for all to see and silencing him for good.

The Lesson

Problem-solving comes in many varieties.

As Sam so eloquently puts it, there are three types of people in this world: "Either you're part of the problem or you're part of the solution, or you're just part of the landscape." I always seek out people who are part of the solution–those who recognize a problem and are geared toward coming up with solutions.

Some people are great at pointing out problems, but it becomes a never-ending loop of rehashing the problem repeatedly. They never take the next step to solving or ending it. People like this can be part of the landscape (or simply exist) due to their ineffectiveness; they can also be part of the problem because they distract the group from finding solutions and waste valuable time.

Then there are people like Spence. They are so locked into the narrative in their own minds that they can't see the flaw in their logic or read the room. They are driven by ego and their need to constantly prove themselves. True collaboration involves people coming together and sharing the best of themselves to achieve a common goal. Individual excellence should not be ignored, nor should it be the main reason for joining a group.

Sometimes, people who are part of the problem don't realize it and need a carefully placed cup of coffee to make them see they are making things worse. Sometimes, those who are a part of the solution need to make sure everyone is included when acting on those solutions. They should avoid trying to be a hero and keep everyone involved in the process, like everyone's got a hand on the wheel.

And sometimes, people are part of the landscape and should ensure their actions–or inactions–are helpful to all involved and don't block progress.

Se7en (1995)

Starring Morgan Freeman, Brad Pitt, Kevin Spacey

The Quote

WILLIAM SOMERSET: *If John Doe's head splits open and a UFO should fly out, I want you to have expected it.*

The Context

When retiring police detective William Somerset tackles a final case with the aid of newly transferred David Mills, they discover a number of grisly murders committed by a serial killer who is targeting people he thinks represent one of the seven deadly sins. Somerset and Mills have been one step behind the killer, John Doe, the entire time. All of a sudden, John Doe appears and wants to take them on a trip they can't refuse. It is clearly a trap, but they have to go along with it to complete the journey. Doe clearly has the upper hand.

While preparing for the doomed mission, the calmer, more seasoned detective offers this advice to his more hot-headed junior partner: "If John Doe's head splits open and a UFO should fly out, I want you to have expected it." Obviously, that specific thing didn't happen, but the point remains the same.

The Lesson

Be prepared for anything.

I live my life accepting that anything can happen and that people are capable of any premeditated or spontaneous action. Many of our poor reactions are due to the expectations we carry with us when we walk into a room. When our expectations are not met (surprise!), we lose our composure and curse the world for its betrayal.

But the key is to understand that rarely will our expectations be met and that we must accept the hand we are dealt. If nothing knocks you off your game, you will be able to respond to what is right in front of you and move forward to the next surprise. That metaphorical UFO popping out of someone's head might be better than what you were expecting.

Scent of a Woman (1992)

Starring Al Pacino, Chris O'Donnell, Gabrielle Anwar

The Quotes

LT. COL. FRANK SLADE: *What life? I have no life! I'm in the dark here. You understand? I'm in the dark!*

LT. COL. FRANK SLADE: *Out of order. I'll show YOU "out of order"! You don't know what "out of order" is, Mr. Trask. I'd show you, but I'm too old, I'm too tired, I'm too fucking blind. If I were the man I was five years ago, I'd take a FLAMETHROWER to this place!*

The Context

Frank is not a happy man. He is old, blind, and retired from the army with nothing to look forward to. He has alienated everyone who ever cared for him. All except Charlie, the kid hired to watch him for the holiday break.

After an emotional adventure through New York City, Charlie helps Frank come to terms with his problems and recognize the positive aspects of his life. Instead of wallowing in self-pity, Frank decides to mount a full-throated defense of Charlie in his own time of need.

The Lesson

Focus less on what you can't do and more on what you can.

If I made two lists—one for what's missing in my life and one for what's going well—the "missing" column would easily win. I suspect I'm not alone. It's so simple to obsess over what we lack. Sometimes that obsession comes from depression; other times we disguise it as ambition so we feel like we're striving toward something.

Take my own list of lamentations: I'm not the captain of a starship (a real disappointment), I've skydived only twice, my right eye refuses to cooperate, and teleportation continues to elude me.

Silly? Maybe. But each one taps into a longing for freedom and purpose that I know I'll never fully grasp.

When those thoughts start to drag me under, I shift the lens to what I *can* do. I can walk, run, explore an entire city, or hop a plane to another country. I get to be on video sets, trusted with crews, and collaborate on stories that didn't exist before we imagined them. We're not charting new star systems, but we are creating new worlds together.

It reminds me of when Charlie shows Frank what he's capable of: "You can dance the tango and drive a Ferrari better than anyone I've ever seen." That spark of camaraderie gives Frank the clarity to defend Charlie—and to face his own flaws.

I have plenty of weaknesses, sure. But I choose to use what I do have to help others and savor each moment. I procrastinate, but I persevere. I'm overweight, but I enjoy every meal and walk it off later. I don't earn much, but I save for what matters.

And yes, I get lonely, but that solitude fuels my gratitude, my creativity, and even pages like this one.

The Quote

LT. COL. FRANK SLADE: *I mean, there's no one who wants to tear a herring with me anymore.*

The Context

Charlie has recently found out that after a tour of pleasures throughout New York City, Frank intends to kill himself. He is having a hard time finding a reason to live. Because he's a military man, he's trained to fight. The problem is that he has become so abrasive and supercilious that no one wants to engage with him anymore.

The Lesson

Find a purpose that keeps you alive.

Frank Slade and my father had more in common than I ever realized when I first watched *Scent of a Woman*. Both were military men through and through. My father served as a trombonist in the Fifth Army Band and was eventually deployed to Vietnam. He carried himself with a kind of abrasive charisma–magnetic at first, but ultimately exhausting. Conversations with him felt like sparring matches. He didn't communicate so much as dominate, wearing people down until they either agreed with him or walked away.

TRIGGER WARNING: SUICIDE

In May 2021, during the long, quiet stretch of the pandemic, my father ended his life in the living room where I grew up–where we watched movies, argued, laughed, and lived. I hadn't seen him in years, though we had spoken on the phone about a month before he died. He was in pain, both physically and emotionally, and long past the point where my encouragement could move him. He was immovable, determined to stay exactly as he was.

Whenever I think of the quote, "There's no one who wants to tear a herring with me anymore," I imagine how my father must have felt near the end. His identity was built on conflict–on pushing, prodding, and trying to shape the people around him. When everyone he sparred with finally stepped away–his family, friends, coworkers–he was left without the purpose that had defined him.

Peacetime, for someone whose life was built on combat–emotional or otherwise–can be terrifying. With pain closing in and no mission left, he may have seen no reason to continue. He left no note, only the quiet signs that he had been preparing for weeks. The guns and ammunition he collected "for safety" became the tools of his own undoing.

I hold no anger, only relief that his suffering is over. His battles began long before I existed, and for years I carried the weight of them. Now I know the burden was never mine.

I just wish he hadn't needed to fight so hard, with himself and everyone else.

Starship Troopers (1997)

Starring Casper Van Dien, Denise Richards, Neil Patrick Harris, Michael Ironside

The Quote

JEAN RASCZAK: *This is for all you new people. I have only one rule. Everybody fights, no one quits. If you don't do your job, I'll kill you myself! Do you get me? Welcome to the Roughnecks!*

The Context

Jonny Rico is part of the mobile infantry of humanity's fight against bugs from another part of the galaxy. He nearly survives the slaughter of the first major offensive of the war. He is reassigned to a new, more organized division called the Roughnecks. The commander of this outfit is revealed to be his former high school teacher, who has only one rule.

The Lesson

Manage everyone's expectations.

Manage expectations of everyone in the clearest and most direct way possible. Everyone enters a job or project with their skills and experience, but may lack awareness of what is expected. The key to success is assessing their skills and guiding them toward the goals of the project. An additional benefit is helping individuals see how their skills fit into the larger group.

In the scenario of *Starship Troopers*, Rasczak singles out the new recruits because the rest of his group is so disciplined that they already know what he expects and what will happen if they don't meet those expectations. He is a great simplifier. He identifies:

- The people he is referring to
- The one rule they need to remember
- What they should and shouldn't do to succeed
- The consequences if they fail
- An acknowledgment of that information

- A confident, straightened-spine greeting to the group, which they repeat without hesitation

A good leader must ensure that everyone is aware of the rules and goals of a project. This includes all who are physically working on the elements of the project (set folks, editors, artists, etc.), everyone managing the process (producers, assistant directors, graphic design and post-production managers, etc.), and those overseeing the process (clients, financiers, CEOs, etc.). Each person should have a clear understanding of how they can contribute to the success of the project and how other areas will support that effort.

If your team has worked together long enough to recite the rules in an immediate call-and-response manner, you have successfully transformed a group of individuals into a passionate team working toward a common goal. Support both the individuals and the group so that everyone brings their best to the team.

Star Trek VI: The Undiscovered Country (1991)

Starring William Shatner, Leonard Nimoy, DeForest Kelley

The Quote

> **CAPTAIN SPOCK:** *Logic, logic, logic. Logic is the beginning of wisdom, Valeris, not the end.*

The Context

This is the final voyage of the original *Star Trek* cast. Spock, who is half Vulcan/half human, has always leaned toward the more logical half in comparison to his friend James T. Kirk. In this particular moment, Spock is talking to a young Vulcan named Valeris, who has displayed exceptional skills. She is fully Vulcan and only has logic as a rudder.

On the surface, their debate is about whether to help an enemy that is on a path to annihilation. Below the surface, they are discussing logic versus faith. Spock argues that, despite his training and beliefs in logic, sometimes we must trust that the universe will unfold as it should. When Valeris presents a familiar reply around how illogical that notion is, he replies, "Logic, logic, logic. Logic is the beginning of wisdom, Valeris, not the end."

The Lesson

Sometimes it takes a lifetime (or two in Spock's case) to understand that no matter how much we try to shape the universe, no matter how much we learn, events will play out how they are meant to. Spock's arc takes him from always presenting the logical path to accepting that his illogical friends can sometimes be right, to finally realizing that the balance between logic and faith is remarkable.

To use food as a metaphor to describe this quote, logic is the recipe, the beginning of the culinary journey. It is essential because it helps us know the ingredients and the order in which they are prepared. But we don't eat recipes. Logic must transform into the actual dish. Real ingredients must be procured and prepared. Heat (or exterior stimuli) must be applied. Sometimes that heat can be controlled, and sometimes it can be unstable. But we work with what we have and apply it to the ingredients for a certain amount of time until the recipe is a finished dish, ready to be consumed.

Recipes alone cannot sustain our hunger, just like logic alone cannot sustain the complexities of life. Recipes pass knowledge from person to person, much like logic. But as life progresses, recipes change and evolve as the users experiment with new ways of cooking the same dishes. We can't control how our recipes are made, only what we do with them. With every choice each chef makes, the recipe evolves. Much like logic, a recipe is the beginning of the journey, not how it ends.

Apply logic at the start, but have faith that the situation you face will take a natural course, and hopefully the result will nourish your soul.

Star Trek: First Contact (1996)

Starring Patrick Stewart, Brent Spiner, Jonathan Frakes

The Quote

CAPTAIN JEAN-LUC PICARD: *I will not sacrifice the Enterprise. We've made too many compromises already; too many retreats. They invade our space, and we fall back. They assimilate entire worlds, and we fall back. Not again. The line must be drawn here! This far, no further! And I will make them pay for what they've done!*

The Context

The starship *Enterprise* has been thrown back in time by a deadly enemy, the Borg. Outnumbered and soon to be overrun, the crew suggests destroying the ship. Its captain, Jean-Luc Picard, rejects this idea. His normally calm head in a dangerous situation is nowhere to be seen here. He has a personal history with the Borg that is influencing his judgment. His anger and rage have reached a boiling point that we, the audience, have never seen.

The Lesson

I have been a fan of Captain Picard's leadership style for as long as I can remember.

The situations the *Enterprise* faced usually followed this pattern: Something puzzling and potentially dangerous happens. The crew reacts and takes steps to stabilize the situation. Picard and his command crew meet at a large conference table. He listens to analyses from each member of the crew about what they think the situation is and what they believe should be done. Sometimes a spirited debate ensues. Once he has heard from everyone, he decides what they should do next. The crew carries out his decision. There is a reaction from that action, and once again, they assemble and repeat the process until the larger problem is resolved.

This is a measured approach to problem-solving that uses collaboration, effective communication, repetition, and the scientific method. Throughout the run of the show and the movies, rarely did Picard lose control of his emotions. When he did, it was an amazing sight, allowing us to study our own breaking points.

We all let our emotions get the better of us. At best, it is a passing moment that will not impact our life or the lives of anyone within earshot. At worst, it can destroy countries, ideas, or even lives. To suppress those feelings is just as dangerous as letting them eat away at our own peace.

It is better to acknowledge your rage without letting it consume you. In this film, Picard had a new friend, Lily, to bring him back from the edge after his (well-deserved) tantrum. She encouraged him to do what was necessary, step back from his rage-filled path, and adopt the more logical approach that had become his trademark. May we all have such a friend in our midst when we declare that "the line must be drawn here" who help us see a better path and move on to the next episode.

The Quote

COMMANDER WILLIAM RIKER: *Someone once said, "Don't try to be a great man. Just be a man, and let history make its own judgments."*

The Context

Dr. Zefram Cochrane is overwhelmed. He has just been told by "astronauts on some kind of star trek" from the future that he will go on to do great things. He doesn't think he is up to the task. Riker shares these words with him, which Zefram thinks are nonsense. Unbeknownst to him, they are his own words, ten years hence.

The Lesson

Don't try to be great. Just be yourself and let your friends, family, and history tell your story (or write a book and tell your own story).

Star Trek: Generations (1994)

Starring Patrick Stewart, William Shatner, Malcolm McDowell

The Quote

CAPTAIN JAMES T. KIRK: *Don't let them promote you. Don't let them transfer you. Don't let them do anything that takes you off the bridge of that ship. Because when you're there, you can make a difference.*

The Context

This is the unlikely meeting of two legendary Starfleet captains: James T. Kirk and Jean-Luc Picard. Though separated by time, they are brought together by an anomaly. Kirk, in this moment, is staring down his greatest foe, retirement. In contrast, Picard is meeting someone who seemingly died decades ago.

The Lesson

We all have to move on at some point.

Kirk is holding onto the past with everything he can. He has found meaning and purpose on the bridge of the *Enterprise*. When they promoted him, he discovered that he had lost a part of himself. His words to Picard, who is in his prime, serve as a warning not to risk losing his own sense of purpose.

It is hard to find where we belong. It's even harder to keep hold of it once we have found it. That kind of purpose is a fragile thing. And when we have served our purpose, there will be forces that will convince us to move on to "better" things. Before accepting that promotion, change of life, or passing of the baton, take stock of what you are giving up in the process. How much of you is rooted in the position you currently hold? Have you truly appreciated it?

All good things come to an end. But try your best not to rush to the next phase. And when that next phase is inevitable, take the lessons and the stories with you and move on with grace. This is how your story was meant to evolve. You might find comfort in connecting with the next generation.

Bonus Quote

STAR TREK II: *The Wrath of Khan (1982)*
SPOCK: *If I may be so bold, it was a mistake for you to accept promotion. Commanding a starship is your first, best destiny; anything else is a waste of material.*

Suicide Kings (1997)

Starring Christopher Walken, Denis Leary, Jay Mohr, Henry Thomas

The Quote

CHARLIE BARRET: *It was your idea, Dunsky!*

The Context

Charlie has been kidnapped, and things are not going well. The kidnappers are idiots who are lying to each other. One of Charlie's men comes to rescue him and shoots one of the kidnappers, Brett, in the leg. When Brett asks why, Charlie responds, "It was your idea, Dunsky!"

The Lesson

Snappy comebacks can focus the point.

With so many twists and turns, I had almost forgotten that Brett was the mastermind. Charlie had a good reason to pick any of his kidnappers to shoot, but Brett was the funniest.

I often use this line to remind people of the seemingly prominent role they're playing in the current situation. People often forget the chaos they trigger, and they need reminding. Why not do it with a humorous, snappy comeback?

Bonus: Using the name "Dunsky" in your snappy comeback is unexpected and not as offensive as more common and recognizable terms.

Tombstone (1993)

Starring Kurt Russell, Val Kilmer, Dana Delaney, Billy Zane

The Quote

JOSEPHINE MARCUS: *Interesting little scene. I wonder who that tall drink of water is.*

MR. FABIAN: *My dear, you've set your gaze upon the quintessential frontier type. Note the lean silhouette … eyes closed by the sun, though sharp as a hawk. He's got the look of both predator and prey.*

JOSEPHINE MARCUS: *I want one.*

MR. FABIAN: *Happy hunting.*

The Context

Josephine and Fabian are stage performers who have just arrived in the Western town of Tombstone. Josephine locks eyes with the legendary Wyatt Earp and immediately wants a frontiersman for herself.

The Lesson

Live as epic a life as possible.

This was my first on-screen crush. Josephine's energy, free spirit, and sensuality captured my attention in a big way. She knew what she wanted and did not apologize for it. She traveled from town to town as an actress. Even though her family was rich, she did what she loved and loved whomever she wanted.

I always hoped that one day a woman like her would take one look at me and say, "I want one." Obviously, people are not possessions, but a person can dream.

The Quote

DOC HOLLIDAY: *I stand corrected, Wyatt. You're an oak.*

The Context

Doc Holiday is making fun of Wyatt because he knows he is attracted to Josephine despite being "kind of" married to Maddie. When asked what Wyatt would do if Josie walked in, he replies that he would ignore her. With comedic timing, Josie enters and dances her way right to Wyatt. She asks for a dance, and he turns to ignore her.

Doc, impressed with Wyatt's fortitude, replies, "I stand corrected, Wyatt. You're an oak."

They meet each other again in the next scene, and Wyatt says, "Yeah, I'm an oak, alright," then begins the process of succumbing to her charms.

The Lesson

Do your best to be an oak.

You can do only so much. Wyatt did his best to prove how strong and virtuous he was. He held his ground and stunned the naysayers. But in the end, we are human, and if we truly want something, like Wyatt wanted Josie, no number of roots will withstand the storm.

The Quote

WYATT EARP: *We've done our good deed for today.*

The Context

Wyatt Earp and his brothers and Doc Holliday are drawn into a conflict with the Clantons and the McLaurys, which comes to a head at a shootout at the O.K. Corral. The Earps and Holiday are victorious, killing three of their enemies.

In the aftermath, Wyatt walks up to the mayor and says, "We've done our good deed for today," as they have done away with evil men.

The Lesson

Recognize the good deeds you perform.

As a producer and a parent, my days are filled with activity. There is always something that needs to be completed, solved, or fixed.

Every once in a while, I'll look up and realize that for a moment I made someone's day better. In that moment, I'll say to myself, "I've done my good deed for today." It is my way of appreciating the good I do in this life.

Sometimes I'm hard on myself and feel that I always have to be switched on. If there is downtime, that is time I am not helping someone and therefore failing at life. I know it is not true, but emotions are not always logical. When this quote comes to mind, I allow myself an internal celebration and rest my soul.

If another opportunity arises to do a good deed within that day, I'll obviously take it. It's only natural for someone who wanted to be Batman. For now, I'll settle for Wyatt Earp. Baby steps.

Twister (1996)

Starring Helen Hunt, Bill Paxton, Cary Elwes, Philip Seymour Hoffman

The Quote

BELTZER: *The average man spends his life avoiding tense situations.*

DUSTY: *Repo Man spends his life getting into tense situations, Beltzer!*

The Context

This is such a fun movie! It follows a wild group of thrill-seeking scientists on a mission to study tornadoes, each with their own unique personality and specialty. They are chasing a tornado when loud rock music blares from their CB radios. It's clear they've worked together for a long time, sharing special calls and responses.

Along for the ride is an outsider, who, like the audience, is experiencing this controlled chaos for the first time. She quickly realizes she has no desire to face the tense situations this group so enthusiastically enjoys.

The Lesson

Tense situations are something to face, not avoid.

I've learned more about people through how they react to tense moments than during calm ones. There's another quote from the television show *Firefly* that hits this point perfectly: "Live with a man for forty years. Share his house, his meals, speak on every subject. Then tie him up and hold him over the volcano's edge, and on that day, you will finally meet the man."

Moments like these can be insightful. You discover a lot about yourself when you're faced with discomfort. Before college, I worked at the theater of the Museum of Contemporary Art. One day, I went up to the catwalk while preparing for a show. It was the first time I was suspended so high in a narrow, dark space. I noticed my tense situation and realized it could be a defining moment. Am I afraid of tight, dark, high places?

As I analyzed the moment, I realized I wasn't the first person to traverse that catwalk, so most likely I wasn't going to fall. Even though it was dark, I still had some ambient light to see. Even though it was tight, it wasn't going to get tighter, and I had a way out. At that moment, I chose not to fear these things, and since then, I've never been afraid of heights, the dark, or tight spaces.

The same applies to many people I've met and worked with over my career. I've learned more about those folks in a tense thirty-minute project meeting than in hours of small talk.

Tense situations can be the best teachers. Recognize the tension in a storm and find a way to use it to your advantage. And most importantly, have fun!

The Vernon Johns Story (1994)

Starring James Earl Jones, Mary Alice

The Quote

VERNON JOHNS: *My daddy always said, "If you see a good fight, get in it."*

The Context

Vernon Johns is a bull-headed African American pastor at the Dexter Avenue Baptist Church in Montgomery, Alabama, in 1948. He and his community are faced with blatant racism and segregation in their daily lives. While some in the congregation preach taking things easy and not antagonizing the white members of the town, Pastor Johns prefers to take a much more direct approach. When confronted about his abrasive nature, he speaks the words of his father.

The Lesson

If it matters, fight for it.

I am not Batman, but I have spent the better part of my time on earth with my eyes and ears open, ready to assist anyone in need. I have picked up and returned dropped items to strangers. I have sat with suicidal friends through the night, making sure they feel valued until they get the proper therapeutic help. When people need help, I respond. Why and how we got here is not essential in the moment. Help first, assess the reasons later.

There is a very important person in my life who taught me by example how to harness this superpower. Her name is Kari. She was my boss for many years, my mentor for even longer, and my friend for life. Though she is a woman, I call her my dad because she taught me so many lessons that he didn't provide. It's not his fault, he wasn't equipped for it. But she filled that role constantly.

Kari is the type of person who helps anyone she encounters. She takes whatever official steps she can and then carefully breaks whatever rule is necessary to get the job done. She truly cares that people are taken care of. That is her good fight to always get into. I was a recipient of her fierce protection program. When I first started working for her in the early 2000s, my pay was massively delayed. Without hesitation she gave me $1,000 of her own money to help me get through the Christmas holiday.

When I think of her and the quote by Vernon's daddy, I am reminded that there is always a good fight nearby and to always get into it. Never pass it by. I am blessed to have received the same assistance time and time again. And that is how I pay it forward.

The West Wing (1999-2006)

Season 1, Episode 19: Let Bartlet Be Bartlet

Starring Martin Sheen, Rob Lowe, Allison Janney, Bradley Whitford, Richard Schiff, John Spencer

The Quote

TOBY ZIEGLER: *It's not the battles we lose that bother me; it's the ones we don't suit up for.*

The Context

The White House staff is battling politically on multiple fronts and sometimes gets trapped in playing it safe. Toby, the communications director, is especially frustrated about the battles they don't take on.

The Lesson

Win or lose, battle for what you believe.

Many people don't get into the fight, make the call, send the email, or speak up because they believe they will lose. It's easy to give in to fear when the outcome seems certain. But nothing is guaranteed. The slightest chance of success is worth taking.

Before I wrote this book, I could never say I was a writer. When I told people I was writing a book, they couldn't believe it because it wasn't in my nature. The chances of this book being finished or even published seemed slim. But if I hadn't "suited up" for the challenge of creating this book, you'd never be reading these words. And I would have regretted not trying more.

Losing can happen. But don't avoid trying just because you might lose. Suit up!

The Quote

Season 1, Episode 22: What Kind of Day Has It Been

PRESIDENT BARTLETT: *What's next?*

The Context

Whenever the president finishes a conversation or it has run its natural course, he says, "What's next?" It's an instinctual remark between him and his staff, not only to keep things moving but also to remind everyone that there's a lot to do for the betterment of the American people.

The Lesson

Find a way to move on.

I used to work for an Edtech company in Redwood City, California, south of San Francisco. The larger coworking building that our company rented space from had a big slide that took you from the second floor to the ground floor. I fell in love with it the moment I saw it–finally, one of those fun Bay Area office perks I'd heard so much about.

The job was challenging, but after a while, I developed a rhythm where I would focus on one thing at a time, be it a lesson plan, a shot list, or a creative idea. As a reward for myself, after finishing that task, I would walk away from my desk triumphantly, slide down the slide like a little kid, and get some air. It was my way of clearing my mind, refreshing my perspective, and coming back recharged, ready for "What's next?"

Everyone should find a way to step away after completing a task and reward themselves, so they can gear up for their next challenge.

The Quote

Season 1, Episode 14: Take This Sabbath Day

PRESIDENT BARTLETT: *The devil you know beats the devil you don't. I like the devil I got.*

The Context

The president is asked to support a new candidate for a specific public office. When he decides to stick with the current holder, he says, "The devil you know beats the devil you don't. I like the devil I got."

The Lesson

Newer is not always better.

Sometimes the grass looks greener on the other side of the fence. But is it really greener? Or better? Sometimes things aren't perfect, and we look for better options. Jobs. Relationships. Power tools. Pubs. The desire for improvement and innovation is a natural part of human nature. But sometimes the unknown can be worse than what we have now. I worked for an organization that had the same leader for years, yet it was widely believed that this leader wasn't right for the organization and needed to be replaced. A search led us to another candidate who, on the surface, seemed like a knight in shining armor. People were practically swooning.

I took a step back to observe and realized that we were all so desperate for authentic leadership that we were willing to settle for anything. The bar was so low that we overlooked the subtle red flags. We quickly hired this new person, and almost immediately the spirit of the organization was tarnished, forcing it to become something it wasn't. With hindsight, we can all agree that it truly worsened the organization, with devastating long-term effects. We should have asked more questions–better questions about what kind of leadership we truly needed and wanted. When red flags appeared, we should have taken a step back, kept what we had, and continued searching for better options.

Stick with what you have until you're as sure as possible that you aren't choosing any devils, past or future. Don't let desperation push you into something worse than what you already have.

The Quote

Season 3, Episode 5: War Crimes

TOBY ZIEGLER: *We're a group. We're a team. From the president and Leo on through, we're a team. We win together; we lose together. We celebrate and we mourn together. And defeats are softened and victories sweeter because we did them together ... You're my guys and I'm yours ... and there's nothing I wouldn't do for you.*

The Context

Someone on the staff leaked a confidential statement made by a senior staffer to a reporter, which will be seen as an embarrassment to the president. Toby demands that everyone on the assistant level who may have leaked the information come in immediately.

Everyone expects Toby to go ballistic (as is his custom) and chain the doors of the White House until the leaker is found. Instead, he has a heartfelt chat with them, saying that while this is a troubling moment, he is not going to hunt for the leaker. He eloquently states that they are a team, that their fates are intertwined, and that there isn't anything he wouldn't do for them.

The Lesson

Earn the right to give this speech.

One of the greatest moments of my life was during training for the 2012 Illinois Leadership Seminar. I had volunteered in various roles since I attended the seminar in 1998 and eventually became the seminar chair. The board and our longtime volunteers nominated and trusted me to run this organization for the year. Two weeks before the actual seminar, we held a training session for new and returning staff.

I had the chance to stand in front of nearly one hundred passionate volunteers and set the stage for the life-changing event about to happen. At the end, I used this quote (making it gender-neutral, of course). It perfectly captured the right tone for that moment and honestly conveyed my feelings. I believe that every team I work with should celebrate and mourn together and share each other's journeys, whether we work together for a weekend or a decade.

When a team works well together, it's the best feeling in the world. Those moments should be honored and cherished. What better way than with a heartfelt and optimistic quote to make the team feel appreciated? This quote truly reflects who I am.

Wyatt Earp (1994)

Starring Kevin Costner, Gene Hackman, Dennis Quaid, Mark Harmon

The Quote

DOC HOLIDAY: *My mama always told me never put off till tomorrow people you can kill today.*

The Context

Wyatt Earp is a legendary lawman who is constantly bound by honor. Doc Holiday is on the opposite side of the law and dying of tuberculosis. Circumstances have brought Wyatt and Doc together to be the closest friend each of them has. When a group of cowboys threatens the life of Wyatt and his brothers, Doc eagerly steps in and counters the threats with one of his own: "My mama always told me never put off till tomorrow people you can kill today."

The Lesson

Solve the problem today.

As a producer one of my best skills is problem-solving. Corporate culture sometimes dictates that when a problem arises, we need to schedule a meeting with the relevant parties to discuss the situation and find a solution. Sometimes that meeting can be days or weeks in the future, depending on schedules. Other times we need to have a meeting to identify the problem, followed by another meeting to discuss a solution, and then another meeting to communicate the solution to everyone involved. It can become an endless loop.

I prefer to examine the problem and then connect with the relevant people as soon as possible to discuss the issue, solve it, and implement a solution. There are times when a problem is discovered in the morning, and after individual conversations, we need to advance the narrative and find a solution to implement by the end of the day. It takes a willingness to seek out the people you need, reading the moment as to whether this is a good time or the problem is significant enough to warrant urgency, and keeping a few conversational plates spinning at the same time.

The goal is to do everything possible to solve the problem today or at least know what we need to do tomorrow to move things forward. Sometimes it can be fun to have so much activity taking place in a corporate environment. But it also serves as a way to take care of today's problems, to make room for tomorrow's, and to avoid compounding the challenges you will inevitably face each day.

In short, Doc Holiday always told me never put off for tomorrow a problem you can solve today.

2000s to 2010s

24 (2001-2010)

Season 7, Episode 1: Day 7: 8:00 a.m.–9:00 a.m.

Season 4, Episode 6: Day 4: 12:00 p.m.–1:00 p.m.

Starring Kiefer Sutherland, Mary Lynn Rajskub

The Quotes

JACK BAUER: *When I am activated, when I am brought into a situation, there is a reason. That reason is to complete the objectives of my mission at all costs.*

JACK BAUER: *I'm not turning back, Erin.*

The Context

Jack Bauer is a federal agent working for the Counter Terrorist Unit. He exemplifies resilience because he will stop at nothing to prevent terrorists' plans and save innocent lives. Often, his own organization and government attempt to stop him with bad information, ineffective leadership, or compromised officials with ambitions as dark as the terrorists'. But Jack refuses to give up, guided by a strict moral code and honoring those who deserve it.

The Lesson

Resilience is a realistic superpower.

When I was in high school, I considered what my preferred superpower would be. It was never superstrength or invincibility. It was *invisibility*. Around my peers, I already felt invisible, as I was not popular or sought out outside of geek and band circles. Sometimes I would do work in the teacher's lounge. The faculty got used to my presence, and I would hear them talk candidly about their jobs and personal lives. There was never anything salacious, but it gave me an opportunity for the first time to hear adults speak honestly. It made me feel invisible yet able to hear the truth.

In my twenties, whenever this superpower question would come up with friends or during random icebreaker games, my answer shifted to teleportation. As a producer on an urban college campus

(Columbia College Chicago) where I had to work and collaborate from one end of the campus to the other, almost a mile away, I walked up and down Wabash Avenue sometimes up to three times a day. I made impossible moments happen because I moved as quickly as I could and talked with everyone involved in the many projects and events I took part in.

In my thirties I tried that same level of coverage, but this time in a car, driving from one side of the San Francisco Bay to the other. I would sometimes traverse San Francisco, Oakland, Berkeley, and Alameda, back to San Francisco—all in one day. After two years of this, I nearly burned out. Yet I still got a lot done during those years, as well as being an anchoring force for my son's first two years on this earth.

The technology to be invisible or teleport doesn't yet exist (as of the writing of this sentence), but now that I am in my forties, I realize I've had a realistic superpower from the beginning.

Resilience is my superpower.

When I sign on, I am in until the action is complete. I always have been. Whether it's managing an event, or a film shoot, hosting or helping at a party, or running a workshop or a family event, I keep going no matter how tired I am or how many twists and turns the day takes. I used to do it to please people, out of fear that I had already let everyone down. These days, I call myself a recovering fixer because, even though I am still extremely resilient, I do it for myself and my own gratification. I choose fewer missions and ones that will fulfill me during and after the journey.

That's likely why I've always admired resilient cinematic heroes like Ethan Hunt (*Mission Impossible*), Dr. House (*House*), Jonas Blaine (*The Unit*), Optimus Prime (*Transformers*), Josiah Bartlett and Josh Lyman (*The West Wing*), Ellen Ripley (*Aliens*), John McClane (*Die Hard*), Joanne Harding (*Contact*), Batman, RoboCop, Dick Tracy, and the most resilient character of all, Jack Bauer (*24*).

When a hero's missions begin, they will do everything possible to fight for what they believe in, regardless of the odds. The one difference between me and these fictional characters is that they are shielded in plot armor, and I am not. But they have inspired me

nonetheless since I was six years old, and I plan to flex my resilience for as long as I possibly can.

I don't have any particular superhero skills, but when I am brought into a project or a job, I do everything I can to get the job done because people are depending on me. Fate has put me in this place and this time, and I want to be known as the person who delivered every time—for the project and for the people who happen to be there.

The Quotes

Season 1, Episode 19: Day 1: 6:00 p.m.–7:00 p.m.
Season 2, Episode 18: Day 2: 1:00 a.m.–2:00 a.m.
Season 3, Episode 19: Day 3: 7:00 a.m.–8:00 a.m.
Season 4, Episode 20: Day 4: 2:00 a.m.–3:00 a.m.
Season 5, Episode 10: Day 5: 4:00 p.m.–5:00 p.m.

SEASON 1: NINA MYERS: *You work for me.*

TONY ALMEIDA: *And you work for Mason.*

SEASON 2: TONY ALMEIDA: *You don't work for Jack; you work for me.*

SEASON 3: TONY ALMEIDA: *She doesn't work for you, Jack; she works for me!*

SEASON 4: BILL BUCHANAN: *You don't work for Jack! You work for me!*

SEASON 5: LYNN MCGILL: *She doesn't work for you, Ms. Raines; she works for me.*

The Context

For the first five seasons of *24*, there was a recurring moment where one character would feel the need to assert who another character does and doesn't work for, essentially reminding them of the command structure.

The Lesson

Noticing patterns can be fun.

Like dogs are acutely aware of sounds from a particular audio register, I am hyperaware of patterns around me. People are predictable—how they speak, how they act in certain situations, how they interact with others. They fall into patterns. I try not to always act on that predictability, as people can intermittently surprise you by breaking the pattern, or our own bias confirms a pattern that doesn't actually exist. But there are patterns all around us.

I derive immense joy from recognizing those patterns. And one joyful moment was when I heard in season 4, "You don't work for Jack, you work for me!" I realized I had heard that line before and then pieced together from memory when it would have taken place in earlier seasons. It was always different people in differing situations, and sometimes the fact that they didn't work for Jack became a common element. I guess this became my version of finding an Easter egg, making the experience that much more joyful.

300 (2006)

Starring Gerard Butler, Lena Headey, David Wenham, Dominic West

The Quote

SPARTAN KING LEONIDAS: *Spartans! Ready your breakfast and eat hearty ... For tonight, we dine in hell!*

The Context

Three hundred Spartans have spent several days holding back an invasion of Greece by the massive Persian army. Outnumbered and now surrounded, they decide to stand and fight to the bitter end. King Leonidas rallies his men with a rousing battle cry: "Ready your breakfast and eat hearty ... For tonight, we dine in hell!"

The Lesson

Set the tone with a well-crafted battle cry.

To inspire your troops, you need to know what motivates them. For some, the thought of dining in hell is enough to make them run as far from the fight as possible. But bad odds and a tough fight are exactly what Spartans were bred for.

Preparation is also crucial. Eating a hearty breakfast, preparing your tools, getting a good night's sleep, reading and understanding the script, practicing your speech, and learning the names and motivations of your team are all ways to prepare for the upcoming activity.

Before a video shoot or event, I talk with each cast and crew member to gauge their mindset. I then arrive early to survey the location. Is it too dark? Is it too noisy? Do we have everything we need to get through the day successfully? Next, I leave the space and take a walk to clear my head and get into the right mindset for the day. It also helps me avoid tunnel vision and remember there's a world outside the microcosm of our production. Finally, once everyone has arrived and settled in, I hold a set briefing and tell them exactly what they need to hear to both inform and energize them.

While I have on several occasions used Leonidas's line to get in the mood, I try to find my own battle cry that fits the moment and unites the cast and crew as one.

Almost Famous (2000)

Starring Billy Crudup, Philip Seymour Hoffman, Patrick Fugit, Kate Hudson

The Quotes

SAPPHIRE: *They don't even know what it is to be a fan. Ya' know? To truly love some silly little piece of music, or some band, so much that it hurts.*

LESTER BANGS: *Music, you know, true music–not just rock 'n' roll–it chooses you. You know, it lives in your car, or alone, listening to your headphones, with vast scenic bridges and angelic choirs in your brain. You know, it's a place apart from the vast, benign lap of America.*

The Context

This story is about the love of music and what it means to be a fan.

The Lesson

Sometimes it's the smallest things that can have the biggest impact.

We don't always get to choose what we fall in love with. A moment can happen that changes our lives and inspires us in ways we may never be able to walk away from.

If you look at an earlier chapter of this book about the movie *The Tall T*, you'll learn how my father heard a single piece of film music that sparked a love resonating through me and led to these pages. He loved film music–more than anything else.

In Shakespeare's play, *Hamlet*, a group of actors visits the castle. To showcase their talent Hamlet asks the older male actor of the group to perform a scene from a play about Hecuba, Queen of Troy. Hamlet is surprised as the actor turns pale and loses all composure when passionately recounting her tragic story. How can this actor evoke enough emotion for someone he doesn't even know to the point where he touches the audience's soul? The idea of a person is strong enough to make feelings real.

The same can be said of music. Existing as sound waves, music is not something tangible you can see or hold. Yet a "silly little piece of music" has the power to push our souls to emotional limits and redefine who we are forever. To push the point further, that piece of music has one meaning for the creator, another for the performer, and countless meanings for everyone it moves.

Whatever inspires you, let it take you to places you never thought possible.

Bad Boys II (2003)

Starring Will Smith, Martin Lawrence

The Quote

MIKE LOWERY: *Hey, you know what would be fuckin' helpful, Marcus? Just shut the fuck up and let me drive, let's try that!*

The Context

Our heroes Mike and Marcus are on a hot pursuit of bad guys who are themselves chasing Marcus's sister. The bad guys have decided to use a big rig with a trailer full of cars as their chase vehicle. As Mike is driving and trying to literally dodge flying cars being thrown at them Marcus is constantly screaming in fear and, in some ways, making the situation worse.

The Lesson

Some people genuinely want to help, but they just can't. Everything they do seems to make the situation worse and distracts you from focusing on solving the problem. I am a problem solver at heart. I'm good at analyzing a situation, figuring out what the problem is, and planning the next steps to get out of it.

I have worked with some amazing problem solvers and learned from them how to handle everything from moving parked cars out of an event lot (with nothing but a furniture dolly and six strong guys) to evacuating a building during a fire. Then there are the people who can't read the situation and refuse to step aside to allow those who are trained or calmer to do what's necessary to save the moment.

To those people, I would love to say, "Hey, you know what would be fuckin' helpful? Just shut the fuck up and let me do this." But I don't. I give people the chance to be part of the solution. And when it's clear they can't, I step in. But just once, I'd like to say those words and see how they react. Life isn't a movie, but how cool would it be if it were?

The Quote

MARCUS BURNETT: *Captain, I was at a family barbecue ...*

The Lesson

A funny cop-out always helps.

I make lots of mistakes, but there have been a few times when I've actually been completely innocent, having nothing to do with whatever went wrong. I wasn't even there. I didn't even know people. "I was at a family barbecue." It's even funnier when I actually was at a family barbecue.

Bonus Quote

CAPT. HOWARD: *I can't believe you guys. Do you get up in the morning, call each other up—"Good morning, Marcus." "Good morning, Mike." "How you doin'?" "Ai'ight." "So, how are we going to fuck up the captain's life today?" "Gee, I don't know, I don't know... Ooh, look! Over there. Let's kill three fat people and leave them on the street?"*

The Lesson

Whatever or whoever is driving you crazy, vent it so you can move forward.

Battlestar Galactica (2004-2009)

Starring Edward James Olmos, Mary McDonnell, Katee Sackhoff, Jamie Bamber

The Quote

ADMIRAL WILLIAM ADAMA: *When you stand on this deck, you be ready to fight, or you dishonor the reason why we're here.*

The Context

Admiral Adama is leading a fleet of ships across the galaxy carrying the last of humanity. They have faced numerous challenges that have resulted in the deaths of hundreds of thousands of people. After a difficult period in their journey, during which he lets down his guard and lives are lost, Adama decides to teach the crew a lesson.

He gets into a boxing ring with his deck chief. The chief thinks it is a friendly match and takes it easy. Adama hits him with full force, causing the chief to realize this fight is real. Adama eventually loses, but he stands, bloody and bruised, and says, "When you stand on this deck, you be ready to fight, or you dishonor the reason why we're here."

The Lesson

Honor the moment and the space by giving your all.

As a producer I have found myself in various sets, stages, meeting rooms, and other locations where a group of us is about to come together to create something that didn't exist before this moment. I love to be the first on set because it's a quiet moment before the storm, when I can gather my thoughts and honor everything that helped me get here. (To learn my full thoughts on how important a space is to me, you can read the entry on *Apollo 13*.)

I encourage everyone to take these kinds of moments seriously. Adama's quote means that when you enter the ring, you take the fight seriously. The same applies to production and creative spaces. Focus is essential to achieving the goals of the project and the career aspirations of everyone involved. Play and joviality are important, but keeping in mind the underlying focus needed to get the job done is the foundation of the moment.

Honor the space you're in. Honor the people you're working with. And when you walk through the door, be ready to get the job done.

Blade II (2002)

Starring Wesley Snipes, Kris Kristofferson, Ron Perlman

The Quote

BLADE: *You obviously do not know who you are fucking with!*

The Context

A bloodthirsty enemy surrounds Blade, and the vampire hunter decides to deliver a definitive one-liner before taking out everyone in the room.

The Lesson

Always take a moment to be a badass. Remind people who you are and then get to work.

The Quote

SCUD: *So, B-man, what do you think?*

BLADE: *Sounds like a plan.*

WHISTLER: *What do you really think?*

BLADE: *They're gonna fuck us the first chance they get.*

The Context

Blade and the vampire nation now share a common enemy. The vampires propose teaming up with Blade and his team, Whistler and Scud. Once they return to their base, Scud asks Blade for his opinion on the plan. At first he responds optimistically. When Whistler presses him further, he then answers honestly.

The Lesson

Manage your own expectations first before shaping the problem for the rest of your team.

As a producer it helps to bring a healthy dose of optimism to the table. It motivates your team and encourages them to face the problem head-on. However, sometimes that optimism can be delusional or lead to underestimating the size of the challenge. That's why well-crafted realism can help manage everyone's expectations.

Everyone works differently and is influenced by different stimuli. Positive reinforcement motivates some people but can be patronizing to others. Realistic assessments can comfort some and frighten others. Over time, through a continuous stream of projects, you can learn the nuances of your team and how to keep them motivated. Adjust your approach so each person receives the information they need to keep moving forward.

Always ensure that as a leader you are aware of and accept the reality of the situation, regardless of the approach you take with your team.

Burn Notice (2007)

Starring Jeffrey Donovan, Gabrielle Anwar, Bruce Campbell, Sharon Gless

The Quotes

The top quotes from this movie, per my friend Spence!

MICHAEL: *You need confidence and a can-do attitude to make it in the field. But if you don't have the physical strength to match your attitude, that confidence can just as easily get you killed.*

MICHAEL: *As a rule, spies don't like dealing with cops. Covert ops are illegal by definition. If they were legal, they wouldn't need to be covert.*

MICHAEL: *For a job like getting rid of the drug dealer next door, I'll take a hardware store over a gun any day. Guns make you stupid; better to fight your wars with duct tape. Duct tape makes you smart.*

The Context

Michael Westen used to be a spy until he received a burn notice, essentially a pink slip from the agency that he has become unreliable and should no longer be trusted. When he was burned, he had nothing: no cash, no credit, no job history. He was stuck wherever they decided to dump him–in this case, Miami.

He did whatever work came his way. He relied on anyone who was still talking to him–a trigger-happy ex-girlfriend, an old friend who used to inform on him to the FBI, family too–because he was desperate. But people needed his help. Bottom line? Until he figured out who burned him, he was not going anywhere.

The Lesson

This chapter is dedicated to my best friend and honorary brother, Spence. I asked him to share his top "as a spy" lessons from *Burn Notice*, because the main character, Michael, is constantly explaining the spy craft he uses to navigate every situation.

Spence has been there for my best moments and my toughest ones. He challenges me to think in ways I never imagined and in ways no one else could. He is a deep thinker and feeler. He pushes himself to question everything and accept nothing at face value. And he is the most confident person I know.

Since we met in 2000, he has introduced me to so many pieces of content I never thought I would enjoy:

- *Firefly* and *Serenity*
- *Cecil B. Demented*
- The music of Aerosmith, Michael Jackson, and Michael Kiwanuka
- The Dead movies (*Dawn of the Dead, Day of the Dead, Night of the Living Dead*, etc.)
- *V for Vendetta*

Our shared love for films like Die Hard and Crimson Tide is boundless. One of the most impactful pieces of content he introduced me to was the show Burn Notice. Many lessons Michael shares carry over into real life. Duct tape truly does make you smart!

Throughout this book, I often refer to how I think "as a producer." That stems from many lessons Michael presents "as a spy." His way of viewing spy craft and how to help or fool people has many parallels with the games a producer must play to bring content to life. Producing is not a straightforward job. Most people don't know what a producer's role actually entails. There's a lot of spy craft involved in the journey from stage to accepting the Best Picture award.

Much of how I think and what I do owes itself to the creativity inspired by *Burn Notice* and Spence's friendship. Like Michael Weston, he does whatever he can to help those in need—whether it's his team members or complete strangers, sometimes at the expense of himself and his mission to find out who burned him.

Spence has never been burned, but he has given much of himself to create amazing art, music, film, and fruitful collaborations that honor the creativity of others.

I love you, Spence. You have shown me new ways to look at film and the world.

The Core (2003)

Starring Aaron Eckhart, Hilary Swank, Stanley Tucci, Delroy Lindo

The Quote

DR. ED "BRAZ" BRAZZELTON: *I don't know what to do!*

The Context

The core of the earth has stopped spinning, and the planet's atmosphere begins to deteriorate. A team of scientists and astronauts embarks on a journey to restart it. Braz has been designing the ship that becomes a key to the mission for over twenty years.

Disaster strikes. One of the ship's compartments is damaged, and it has been established that "one damaged compartment threatens the entire ship." But one of the crew members is trapped in that compartment. The choice is to save either him or the world. Braz pulls open a panel and starts tearing apart wires to open the door. But as he wrestles with the decision, with alarms blaring and other crew members shouting, he breaks down and says to himself, "I don't know what to do."

The Lesson

Acceptance is emotionally efficient, but it takes practice and resilience for us humans to master.

This moment broke my heart. Braz is one of the smartest people on the planet. He is riding his own invention to the center of the earth to fix the problem and save everyone on the planet. He has prepared for every possible scenario and even developed a new metal to cover the ship. But he didn't know he would hold his friend's life in his hands. Nothing can prepare a person for that moment.

Braz breaks down in tears and utters the one phrase so many seek to avoid. Sometimes the road isn't clear. The path is muddy. On top of the tough choices we face, we have our own emotions to deal with. Sometimes we need to stop trying to outsmart fate and admit that we just don't know what to do. It can be sad and a blow to our ego and intellect, but such an admission helps us remember we are human and that some situations are beyond our control.

Braz was not able to make the choice, but the decision was already made for him by the situation. His friend was going to die. He had to die for the mission to continue. His grief in that moment was an outward expression of him fighting with the reality he already knew.

Sometimes we know the answer, but our resistance to it can cause more pain than accepting the choice upfront.

The Dark Knight (2008)

Starring Christian Bale, Heath Ledger, Aaron Eckhart, Michael Caine

The Quote

THE JOKER: *Does it depress you, commissioner? To know just how alone you really are?*

The Context

The Joker has been captured. Commissioner Gordon is questioning him in a dark room. Unfazed by his situation, The Joker manically hints that some of Gordon's people might not be loyal. Given his successful plans so far, the idea that more trouble could come and he doesn't know who to trust is, in a word, frightening.

The Lesson

Being alone and feeling alone are entirely different feelings to protect against.

I grew up in a house by myself. Once I was old enough to be on my own without a babysitter, I was home every Saturday and Sunday night, and summers every Thursday and Friday daytime, as those were the times when my parents' work overlapped. When my parents finalized their divorce, I unfortunately lived with my father, which brought even more loneliness. For almost ten years, movies were my friends. In high school, I spent time in after-school clubs so I could spend more time with people and less time at home.

I was alone all that time, but I never truly felt lonely. It wasn't until years later, during the third trimester of my wife's pregnancy with our only son, that I felt loneliness. We had recently moved from my hometown, Chicago, to San Francisco, a new and strange place where we had few friends. I was trying to find my path. When we got pregnant, there were several milestones to celebrate: the positive test, the changes in my wife's body, the ultrasound, the kicks and punches, and the nesting.

But all of that newness takes place during the first and second trimesters. Depending on the health of everyone involved, it is a balance of worry that something could go wrong and confirmation that all is right. Once we hit the third trimester, there was nothing to do but sit and wait for something to happen.

My whole world was about to change forever in ways that could not be accurately predicted, and there was nothing I could do in the meantime. I had projects and coworkers, but for some reason, I didn't have anyone to connect with on a personal level, given that my wife worked almost completely up until the birth. It was at that time that the Joker's words continually rippled through my brain. It did depress me knowing how alone I was, or more accurately, how alone I felt.

When your friends and family are undergoing massive life changes, it can seem as if it is a happy occurrence. But humans have a way of feeling more alone than they truly are and not being aware of the support that can be activated. Anyone can feel alone, even in a crowd.

Isolation can take many forms. Try your best to check in on the people you care about. You never know what misguided movie quote may be rippling through their brains. Let them know they don't have to be alone or feel lonely.

The Quote

BRUCE WAYNE: *Gotham needs its hero. And I let that murdering psychopath blow him half to hell.*

The Context

Batman did everything he could to save Harvey Dent from the Joker's nefarious plans. But the Joker was always a few steps ahead of everyone, and Dent became mortally wounded. Defeated, Bruce tells Alfred that Dent, the person he thought could do more good than he himself could as Batman, was his responsibility and that he failed to protect him.

The Lesson

Failure is inevitable. Keep going.

Everything we do in this life has a chance of failing. Every business we start, test we take, relationship we begin, creative endeavor we launch, partnership we build, journey we undertake, mission we accept, friendship we nurture, trees and plants we plant, or effort we undertake could fail in many ways. It doesn't matter how much money you have, the skills you bring, the collaborators you gain, or the followers you acquire. History is full of failures. Everyone will fail at something. The first step is accepting that success is not guaranteed.

The key is to be prepared for failure and resilient if it occurs. Examine every aspect of what you're trying to achieve. While hope and optimism are critical for the survival of any endeavor, it helps to consider how it might fail and to prepare yourself as much as possible. Hopefully, the damage can be contained and learned from and you can fail your way to future success. Don't give up your cape and cowl. Accept that you did your best and move on to the next challenge.

Bruce bet everything on the goodness of Harvey's crusade. But as we know, the battle for Gotham's soul did not end with Harvey's disfigurement. Batman carried on and found new ways to thwart the Joker. Hopefully you never have to choose between blowing up a ferry full of innocent people or being blown up by that same group. And whatever you do, don't be the person who puts others in that situation. It's not nice.

The Quotes

TWO-FACE: *You thought we could be decent men in an indecent time.*

COMMISSIONER GORDON: *The Joker took the best of us and tore him down.*

The Context

In a battle for Gotham's soul, Batman and Gordon bet everything on the idea that Harvey Dent was the white knight the city needed and that his goodness would help bring the city back from the brink. In the end, the Joker turned that goodness against all of them and nearly broke the city completely.

The Lesson

Good people can do bad things, and vice versa.

I used to believe that being good was enough–that doing the right and good things was all I needed, and good things would come my way. Sadly, that's not how the world works. Bad things happen to good people, and good things happen to bad people. It's all a big gray area sometimes.

Although my intentions have always been to make life better for anyone I meet, I have upset many. My father was always angry with me, no matter what I did right. My ex-girlfriend in high school was so mad at me that she ignored me at prom. My college girlfriend suffered from deep depression, no matter how much I tried to help her enjoy life. Our breakup was devastating, but I believed it was best for both of us.

No matter how much good I do, it won't always be seen as positive. That's because I cannot control how others view my actions or how the ripples of those actions crash against distant shores. Instead of striving to be good for all humankind and avoiding anything bad, I realize all I can do is simply be. I hope my actions have a positive impact, and if not, at least they don't leave lasting negative effects.

I know I am not the Joker, creating chaos. I have always dreamed of being Batman. But in the end, I am more like Jim Gordon, the Commissioner of the Gotham City Police Department and one of

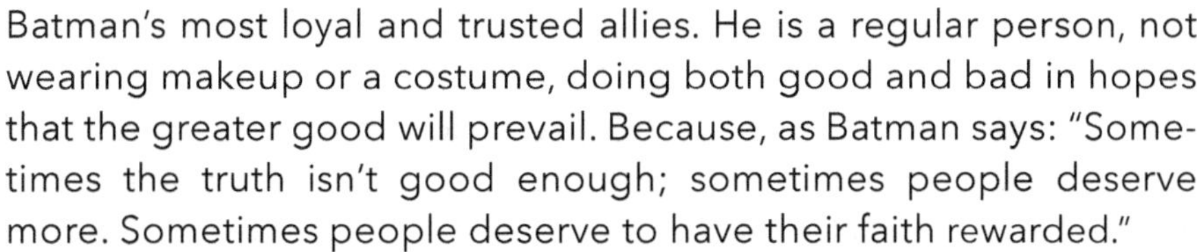

Batman's most loyal and trusted allies. He is a regular person, not wearing makeup or a costume, doing both good and bad in hopes that the greater good will prevail. Because, as Batman says: "Sometimes the truth isn't good enough; sometimes people deserve more. Sometimes people deserve to have their faith rewarded."

Gladiator (2000)

Starring Russell Crowe, Joaquin Phoenix, Connie Nielsen, Oliver Reed

The Quote

PROXIMO: *So, Spaniard, we shall go to Rome together and have bloody adventures. And the great whore will suckle us until we are fat and happy and can suckle no more. And then, when enough men have died, perhaps you will have your freedom.*

The Context

Maximus, or "Spaniard," as he is called by his trainer Proximo, was a celebrated Roman general. He was betrayed by the emperor and left for dead. He survived and is now a gladiator fighting for Proximo. His past is unknown to Proximo. They have been called to perform in the Colloseum where long ago, Proximo won his freedom.

Proximo tries to persuade Maximus to win over the crowd so he can stand in front of the emperor and earn his freedom. They share the same goal but for very different reasons. Proximo, excited to return to Rome, delivers this passionate speech as if they are on an epic journey.

The Lesson

Every journey brings you closer to your future self.

On a recent trip to Rome, this quote came to mind. While no one had to die for me to gain my freedom, I saw the trip as epic. It didn't disappoint. I see every shoot day as a battle to be won, but I view every trip as an epic journey where I will discover more about myself.

As someone who has an identity assigned to him, I see every day as a chance to earn the right to be myself–to be who I am, not who I was meant to be. The epic quote about "bloody adventures" is my way of enjoying the freedom I continue to celebrate.

The Quote

LUCILLA: *I am tired of being strong.*

The Context

Lucilla is the sister of Emperor Commodus. Their father admired Lucilla for her strength and resilience. Commodus is amoral and was not suited to be the emperor. As a result, Lucilla has had to remain tough to hide her disdain for her brother and her love for his rival Maximus, and most importantly, to protect her son.

While Lucilla is planning to end her brother's reign, Maximus comments that she has been strong for everyone she cares about. She lets out a heavy sigh and says, "I am tired of being strong."

The Lesson

Resilience is costly.

When people hear about the difficult parts of my story, they often remark how strong I am. I believe it's out of kindness or sympathy. Many people carry heavy burdens, some visible and others hidden. For the visible ones we cheer, raise funds, start foundations for, and try to pass laws to support recovery and prevention.

The unseen burdens are very hard to support. As the saying goes, you never know what someone is going through, so be kind. We assume that those who seem strong are actually strong and can handle anything. When we first meet Lucilla, she appears to be a spoiled brat. But as the story unfolds, we see her behind-the-scenes actions that make her a trustworthy force for good. It's in moments like these that we see the toll such strength can take.

I've always felt that my ideal superpower, if asked, would be invisibility or teleportation. Being anywhere and everywhere would

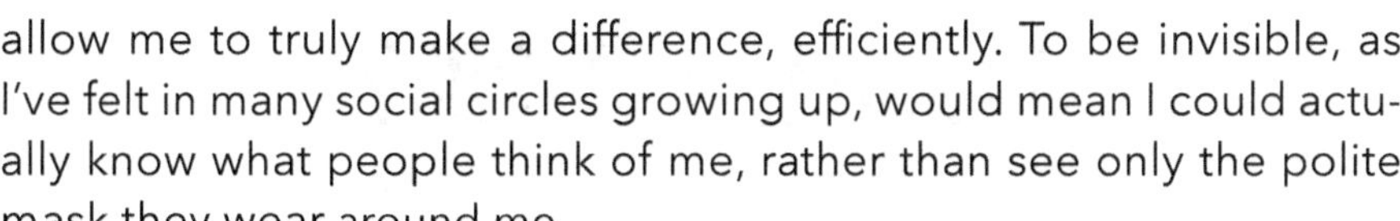

allow me to truly make a difference, efficiently. To be invisible, as I've felt in many social circles growing up, would mean I could actually know what people think of me, rather than see only the polite mask they wear around me.

It took me a long time to admit that my true superpower is resilience. And not because I chose it, but because that resilience was necessary just to get through each day and start the next. I didn't choose this life or my parents. I had no say in whether they should have become a couple. I'm glad they endured, or I wouldn't exist. And I like existing.

But I am dealing with the hand I was dealt. With this hand, it takes resilience to understand myself, navigate the wonderful and difficult people I meet, and work through many challenges. My resilience is part of who I am. Still, even Superman gets tired. It took me too long to realize that I am not Superman and that I would love not to have to be strong for a while.

As a parent you don't have a choice. You have to be many things at any given moments whether you want to or not. Now, I choose what I want to be strong for. I am no longer trying to be everything to everyone. I am not a Swiss Army knife that can handle every situation. I am not a superhero. I know what I can do and what I cannot. I focus on what's essential to me so that I don't exhaust my soul. And when I reach the point where I say, "I am tired of being strong," I will know that I am tired for the right reasons–my reasons. And I will be grateful to myself for the energy I've spent on truly being myself.

House (2004-2012)

Season 3, Episode 12: One Day, One Room

Starring Hugh Laurie, Robert Sean Leonard, Omar Epps, Jennifer Morrison, Katheryn Winnick

The Quote

EVE: *I'm going to base this moment on whom I'm stuck in a room with. That's what life is. It's a series of rooms, and who we get stuck in those rooms with adds up to what our lives are.*

The Context

On the surface, Dr. Gregory House is an angry yet brilliant diagnostician who treats his patients like cases from a Sherlock Holmes mystery. Beneath that, he questions everything in an effort to protect himself from emotional and physical pain. In this moment, he is "stuck in a room" with a patient he slowly discovers has been raped.

What follows is less about solving a medical mystery and more about a philosophical debate designed to encourage her to open up and discuss what happened. He is the only person she will talk to, and he is the last person suited to handle someone in an emotional state. He starts the series never visiting or meeting with his patients. Now he is deeply involved in an emotionally charged moment with someone he would have never accepted as a patient to begin with.

The Lesson

This quote had a profound effect on me. We spend every moment of our lives in a space–whether it's a room, a vehicle, or the personal area we inhabit outdoors–either alone or with others. Even in a world where we are more digitally and virtually connected than ever before in human history, we still invite people into our space and share moments with them.

Every memory we have involves sharing space with either another person or ourselves. Sometimes the people we share space with are chosen by us. Other times we have no choice, like on a train or at work. We never know when we walk into that space how those moments will affect us. We might walk into a room one way and leave feeling completely different, or even have our world changed forever.

Most of the time, nothing dramatic happens and our lives go on, maintaining the status quo. But a single chance encounter on the train can lead to a new relationship or leave us in pain. That one time you walk into your boss's office could mean a promotion or the loss of your job. Our lives are shaped by the rooms we've been in and the people we've shared them with.

I've always actively chosen to be in rooms with people who make my life better. Of course, we can't always choose the people. When I can't, I try to explore the space, be aware of who I'm sharing it with, and remain open to the possibilities those people might bring. Usually we leave those rooms unchanged. But isn't it wonderful when we leave a room better than when we entered?

Think a little deeper about the rooms you're in and who you're stuck with.

Season 6, Episode 21: Help Me

The Quote

> **DR. HOUSE:** *That's the point. I did everything right, she died anyway. Why the hell do you think that would make me feel any better?*

The Context

Dr. House is trying to save a patient trapped under a collapsed building. He's torn between amputating her crushed leg or not, knowing that either way, he'll risk making things worse. He decides to go ahead with the amputation, but in the ambulance the patient suffers a fatal embolism and dies. Dr. House's colleague, Foreman, is concerned that Dr. House blames himself for her death. Meanwhile, Dr. House feels that even though he made the right call, it ultimately didn't matter.

The Lesson

Everyone is so obsessed with right and wrong that we often believe everything we do is right just because we did it. We only think it was wrong because of the real or imagined consequences of our actions. It's all just a matter of perspective–what's right to one person might be wrong to another. One person's revolutionary is another's terrorist. One person's partner is another's betrayer. One person's introvert might be another's extrovert.

You can do everything right and still not get the outcome you want. You can do everything wrong and still experience good things. Dr. House did everything he was trained and skilled to do, yet life found its own way, and the woman he tried to save still died.

Hustle & Flow (2005)

Starring Terrence Howard, Taraji P. Henson, DJ Qualls

The Quote

SHELBY: *Every man has the right, the goddamn right, to contribute a verse.*

The Context

DJay, a pimp in Memphis struggling with a midlife crisis, has joined gospel music producer Key, a prostitute named Nola, and Shelby, an eccentric white man, to create new music inspired by DJay's life experiences. After a magical moment, Shelby decides it's time for a celebratory smoke, during which he expounds on the rights that every man has. "Every man has the right, the goddamn right, to contribute a verse."

The Lesson

Everyone has a voice to use.

Everyone has ideas to share.

Everyone has a piece of their soul that should see the light of day and be appreciated by those it touches.

Everyone deserves to be seen, heard, felt, and experienced.

Everyone has the right to have their existence acknowledged.

Never silence your voice, because you have the right to contribute a verse to the song of human history.

Inside Man (2006)

Starring Denzel Washington, Clive Owen, Jodie Foster

The Quote

KEITH FRAZIER: *I got news for you. Most of the guys up in Sing Sing weren't murderers until they killed somebody.*

The Context

Keith Frazier is a hostage negotiator trying to save people from the strangest bank robbery ever. Many things are not as they seem, and he is working to solve the puzzle. While talking to an associate about how the bank robber doesn't seem capable of murder, he fires off this line to counter the point.

The Lesson

We are all capable of both great and terrible things.

This quote helped me realize that everyone begins at zero when they are born; they don't do anything until they try it for the first time. Everyone has a first step, whether it's a kiss, a day of school, a new friend, a drive, a job, or even trying a new food. Most of the choices we make are also new experiences. Rent or buy. Casual or serious. Walk or drive. Our lives are full of firsts.

Sadly, we also experience our first negatives. We can break someone's heart for the first time, steal, lie, make wrong decisions, unintentionally kill plants (I've killed too many cacti to count), or, in this quote's context, harm others.

We often assume that good people are always good and bad people are always bad, believing there's no way good people would do bad things and vice versa. But in reality, we are complex beings, and life isn't so black-and-white.

Our lives are full of complicated firsts. The key is understanding the consequences of these firsts and recognizing that anyone can do anything if they justify it in their own mind. Stay hopeful, but be prepared for anything.

King Arthur (2004)

Starring Clive Owen, Keira Knightley, Mads Mikkelsen, Ioan Gruffudd, Stellan Skarsgård

The Quote

LANCELOT: *I will die in battle; that I am certain of. But I hope to die in a battle of my choosing. But if it is to be this one, do not bury me in our sad little cemetery. Burn me, and cast my ashes to a strong eastern wind.*

The Context

Arthur and Lancelot are contemplating the meaning of freedom on the eve of their final battle for Rome. Even after death, Lancelot desires to be free.

The Lesson

After watching multiple movies and TV shows where characters and the audience experience what it's like to be buried alive, I decided that I don't want to be buried when I die. I've always been drawn to adventure and exploring new places. There are so many lands to visit and waters to swim in. I used to daydream about what it would feel like to touch a cloud, which led me to go skydiving. I know I will never see every part of this earth, so it seems a waste to be buried in it.

Like Lancelot, I want to be cremated. I want my ashes to explore places I never got to see while alive, carried by the wind. I believe death is a freedom that cannot be taken away, and I want to fly, float, and explore forever.

The Quotes

CERDIC: *Wherever I go on this wrenched island, I hear your name. Always half whispered, as if you were ... a god. All I see is flesh, blood. No more god than the creature you're sitting on.*

CERDIC: *Ahhh, finally, a man worth killing.*

The Context

Cedric, the leader of the Viking army who is pillaging and plundering his way through the lands of Britain, is bored. His army is facing very little resistance, and the natives he allows to live turn against his own people. When he approaches Hadrien's Wall, the gates open and a man on horseback emerges–a man whose name he has heard constantly since they landed in Britain. This man directly challenges him, offering a challenge worthy of his warrior spirit. He gives him a man worth killing. When Arthur finishes his brave ultimatum and turns away, Cedric beats his chest with warrior joy and prepares his troops for battle.

The Lesson

Find a fight worthy of your fight.

When I worked on Columbia's campus, I always imagined that one day someone would approach me and say, "Wherever I go on this wrenched campus, I hear your name. Always half whispered, as if you were ... a god. All I see is flesh, blood. No more god than the pavement you are walking on."

It was actually true because I was well-known and useful across the campus. It was a huge ego boost that a little nerd growing up in a sheltered childhood was of use to incredibly smart college staff, faculty, and students, all doing amazing things. I was everywhere, helping everyone on a large number of projects.

When I finally left Columbia and moved to San Francisco, I drove all over the city doing everything for everyone, making myself indispensable along the way. When I decided I was stretching myself too thin for little benefit, I realized I needed to pick fewer, more impactful fights to wage.

When I sign on to a project worthy of my soul, I take a step back, beat my chest, take a deep breath, and say, "Finally, a fight worth fighting."

Bonus Quote

ARTHUR: *Knights! The gift of freedom is yours by right. But the home we seek resides not in some distant land; it's in us, and in our actions on this day! If this be our destiny, then so be it. But let history remember that as free men, we chose to make it so!*

The Kingdom (2007)

Starring Jamie Foxx, Jennifer Garner, Chris Cooper, Richard Jenkins

The Quote

FBI DIRECTOR JAMES GRACE: *You know, Westmoreland made all of us officers write our own obituaries during Tet, when we thought The Cong were gonna end it all right there. And, once we clued into the fact that life is finite, the thought of losing it didn't scare us anymore. The end comes no matter what, the only thing that matters is how do you wanna go out, on your feet or on your knees? I bring that lesson to this job. I act, knowing that someday this job will end, no matter what. You should do the same.*

The Context

A terrorist attack targeting Americans has occurred in Saudi Arabia. The FBI wants to deploy a task force to properly investigate the crime, but faces political obstacles. Waiting risks the destruction of evidence and the suspects escaping justice. Director of the FBI, James Grace, sends the team anyway, drawing the anger of the attorney general, who plans to "bury" Grace. He then calmly reflects on the lesson he learned in Vietnam and how he applies it to his current work.

The Lesson

All things come to an end. How you face the end is what's important.

It is this very quote that inspired me to write this book. All of us hold on to the status quo with every fiber of our being. We don't want this job, this project, this moment, this kiss, to end. We want things to stay the way they are because they are comfortable and safe. The AG wanted to follow proper procedure because it was politically safe, despite the perpetrators possibly escaping.

Grace's story stuck with me because it made me realize that all things come to an end. Every job I have ever had has ended at some point. Every relationship I have ever had or will have has ended or will end at some point. How I conduct myself during those projects or relationships is more important than trying to make them last. The choices we make are what define us in the end. And the end will come no matter what. Even our lives will end. It's better to apologize for doing what you believe than to ask for permission.

Live Free or Die Hard (2007)

Starring Bruce Willis, Justin Long, Timothy Olyphant

The Quote

JOHN MCCLANE: *Well, the car's on fire. That can't be good.*

The Context

John McClane teams up with a young hacker to stop a cyberterrorist who is launching a massive digital attack on US infrastructure.

In an effort to keep his teammate safe, he is chased into a tunnel and cornered by a helicopter. He decides the best option is to launch a car at the helicopter. As he gets closer, the bad guys in the helicopter shoot at the car, causing the hood and engine to explode. Before jumping out, he says the obvious to himself, "Well, the car's on fire. That can't be good." He bails out, the car lifts off the ground, and ... wait for it ... he takes down the helicopter.

The Lesson

Stating the obvious can help you understand—or at least enjoy—the situation.

The Lord of the Rings: The Return of the King (2003)

Starring Elijah Wood, Viggo Mortensen, Ian McKellen, Orlando Bloom, Bernard Hill

The Quote

THÉODEN: *Arise! Arise, Riders of Théoden! Spears shall be shaken, shields shall be splintered! A sword day … a red day. … ere the sun rises!*

The Context

The armies of man have gathered their forces to battle with the forces of evil. Outnumbered and facing dark, unpredictable magic, their spirits are shaken. It is up to the newly resurrected King Théoden to rally the courage of his men (and woman) and lead them toward what might be certain death.

The Lesson

Go for epic!

I love making music videos. One day, an entire cast and crew were up at the crack of dawn, chatting in the WhatsApp group as we all headed to the location. As the sun was rising, this special speech came to mind. I decided to send the YouTube clip to the group. Those who were receptive to the sentiment were just as pumped as I was.

When the day ended, we realized we had achieved something epic. We created something that didn't exist before, and we did it together. Cameras were rolling! Doubts were shattered! A creative day–a successful day–and there we were, victorious!

Make every day an epic battle to be won. It turns boring days into exciting adventures and exciting days into figurative conquests.

Madagascar (2005)

Starring (voices) Ben Stiller, Chris Rock, David Schwimmer, Jada Pinkett Smith, Tom McGrath

The Quote

SKIPPER THE PENGUIN: *You, quadruped. Sprechen Sie Englisch?*
MARTY THE ZEBRA: *I sprechen.*
SKIPPER THE PENGUIN: *What continent is this?*
MARTY THE ZEBRA: *Manhattan.*
SKIPPER THE PENGUIN: *Hoover Dam! We're still in New York! Abort! Dive! Dive! Dive!*

The Context

A group of penguins is trying to escape from the New York City Zoo. As they are tunneling, they stop and rise to periscope depth to check their progress, only to discover they haven't gotten very far.

The Lesson

This one is for my son. He's eleven now, but when he was three and four years old, we always used to say, "I sprechen," which mildly annoyed my wife, who actually speaks German.

Whenever we playfully expressed shock and amazement, we would say, "Hoover Dam! We're still in New York!" He liked the line immediately. But once I explained that the Hoover Dam was in Nevada, the line became funnier for both of us.

My son and I are on a wonderful journey together, and I love every moment of it. I've always been the kind of person who lives in the present, enjoying each moment as it comes. I don't look back and wish I could relive the past, like some parents do. Right now, he's at a great age, and it feels like it's the best one yet. But quotes like this one bring me back and remind me to cherish the special moments in his life.

Even though he's nearly a teenager now, every once in a while when I say, "Sprechen Sie Englisch?" I'll grudgingly get an "I sprechen" in return. I'll take what I can get and love it.

Man on Fire (2004)

Starring Denzel Washington, Dakota Fanning, Christopher Walken

The Quote

RAYBURN: *A man can be an artist … in anything. Food, whatever. It depends on how good he is at it. Creasy's art is death. He's about to paint his masterpiece.*

The Context

Creasy is a former military operative turned bodyguard. After the child he's protecting is kidnapped and murdered, he seeks out everyone involved. When the police question his friend Rayburn, he provides them with crucial insight into Creasy.

The Lesson

Some people excel at one thing, while others excel at many.

I have always admired people who seem to have answered a calling, as if there was nothing else they could have done with their lives. Anthony Bourdain, John Williams, Lucille Ball, Denzel Washington, Stevie Wonder, Annie Leibovitz, and many more perfected their craft to the point where they became their art.

My first job as a teenager was as a busboy at a restaurant where my mother worked. It had a family vibe, with everyone knowing each other. The best part of the job was that I could enjoy BLTs whenever I was on break–bacon on tap. It was heaven for someone who loved bacon.

One day, one of the cooks told me I was a jack-of-all-trades. I had never heard the term before. He saw my confusion and explained it was a good thing–that I could do anything or jump in at any point to be of service. I wore that compliment like a badge of honor.

It took me a while to hear the rest of the phrase: "A jack-of-all-trades, a master of none." Because I was able to do many things fairly well, I initially felt like I would never master one. At first, I felt like a failure. But after a few years, I realized that the world is too vast and there are too many experiences to have just by doing one thing, especially before age twenty.

I have done many things well. I have achieved greatness in only a few. But my story isn't over. My future self could become a master artist of one specialty. For now, I am content with painting my masterpiece using many different brushes.

The Matrix Reloaded (2003)

Starring Keanu Reeves, Laurence Fishburne, Carrie-Anne Moss, Gloria Foster, Collin Chou

The Quote

SERAPH: *You do not truly know someone until you fight them.*

The Context

Neo is on his way once again to see the Oracle in an effort to understand his fate. This time, he encounters Seraph, the one who is charged with protecting the Oracle, unbeknownst to Neo. Seraph fights Neo to learn his true identity and nature. After the fight, Neo says that Seraph could have just asked who he was, to which Seraph replies, "You do not truly know someone until you fight them."

The Lesson

Find a way to understand the true nature of the people you meet.

While I do not advocate fighting as a means of introduction, there's something to be said for getting to know someone by doing what you enjoy. It takes you out of your head and reveals who they really are and what they're capable of.

I usually meet new people during the preproduction of a project. Words are always exchanged about what to expect from their conduct and character. But it's not until you're in the thick of things that you truly see what they're made of. In hour eleven of the fifth day of filming, after numerous setbacks, people tend to shed the performative facade they had during the job interview and reveal their true selves. Will they be the rock their peers need, or will they exacerbate the problems?

Everyone tries to put their best foot forward initially, whether in job interviews, on first dates, during project briefings, at networking events, or with friends introducing friends. It's inevitable that we meet people and have to decide whether we want to continue building a connection. We can use every observation to weigh the options, but we're still taking a chance on them. Be prepared to meet the real person once things get tough. They might be exactly who they appear to be, or they could be hiding their true self during calmer times. Be prepared.

The Quote

THE ORACLE: *Because you didn't come here to make the choice, you've already made it. You're here to try to understand* why *you made it.*

The Context

Neo is trying to understand the nature of his existence from the Oracle. Instead of giving clear answers, she presents paradoxes in the hope that he will figure it out on his own. At this moment, he is trying to grasp a choice she claims he has already made, yet he still struggles with it.

The Lesson

We will inevitably face choices we struggle to understand.

Making choices is a fundamental part of being human. Do I

- turn left or right?
- scold or compliment?
- go to school or travel?
- go to Italy or Australia?
- sleep with him or not?
- vote Republican or Democrat, Tory or Labour?
- be responsible or have fun?
- propose or keep dating?
- divorce or stick it out?
- buy the ice cream or not?
- write this book or watch another movie?
- lie or tell the truth?

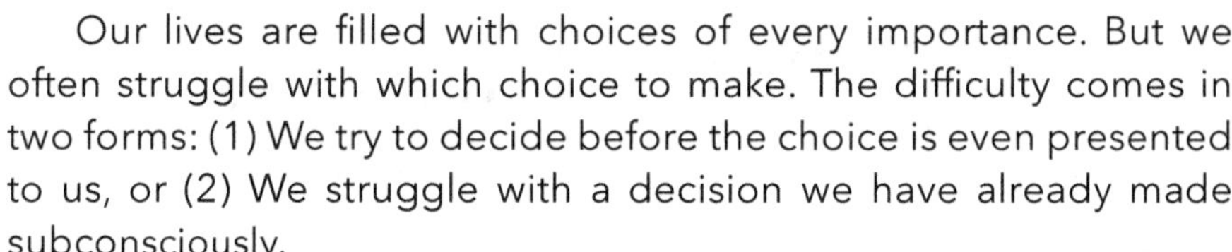

Our lives are filled with choices of every importance. But we often struggle with which choice to make. The difficulty comes in two forms: (1) We try to decide before the choice is even presented to us, or (2) We struggle with a decision we have already made subconsciously.

I observe the first scenario often with elections. We frequently ask, "If the election were today, who would win?" and then generate news stories based on that. But the election isn't today; it's on Election Day. That's the only day we should ask that question. Until then, we should gather as much information as possible to make an informed decision when the time comes.

With the second, and sticking with the election metaphor, most of us already know who we're going to vote for. Once candidates are officially in the race, their policies, beliefs, and character are well-known. Yet we struggle with the choice we've already made.

The person wondering whether they should study abroad or stay in their hometown with their partner and family has already made a decision. They should spend their time accepting that choice and understanding why they made it.

On September 6, 2001, I chose to leave my father's home and venture into an unknown life. Before that, I thought I was struggling with the decision to leave because I had no idea how I could survive without him. In reality, I had already made the choice to live without him over a year earlier, because I knew I could no longer live with him. The decision was made—I just had to understand and accept why I chose it and take the next step.

Ask yourself: Have you already made the choice you're wrestling with? Or is your mind battling over a decision so far in advance that the full scope of that choice hasn't yet emerged? Whether you should accept the job is a good question, but it's premature to debate that before you've even been offered it or interviewed for it. Many decisions depend on others' actions before you can make your own.

Try not to stress over choices that aren't yet in your path. And when they are, don't waste time debating which way to go. You've already made your choice. Now is the time to understand it.

Michael Clayton (2007)

Starring George Clooney, Tom Wilkinson, Tilda Swinton

The Quote

ARTHUR EDENS: *I had the most stunning moment of clarity … And you know what I did? I took a deep cleansing breath, and I set that notion aside. I tabled it. I said to myself, as clear as this may be, as potent a feeling as this is, as true a thing as I believe that I have witnessed today, it must wait. It must stand the test of time. And Michael, the time is now.*

The Context

Arthur Edens is a lawyer at a powerful firm who, while defending a despicable client, experiences a profound moment of clarity about his actions. This realization forces him to question his professional life and take drastic, life-changing steps to be "born anew."

The Lesson

Don't be afraid of the next step.

When I first watched *Michael Clayton*, I had no idea what to expect. I was hooked immediately as a manic voice hurriedly told its story to Michael. No preamble, just a story about breaching the chrysalis.

I've had several moments in my life when I've looked back at where I was and then looked forward, realizing that the next step I took would change my world:

- During the last band performance of my senior year in high school, when my band director, Mr. McClellan, finally, agreed to handle the baton and conduct
- When I decided to leave my father's home.
- When I was on the catwalk high above the Museum of Contemporary Art performance center, and I decided I was not going to be afraid of heights, the dark, or tight spaces.
- When the documentary I produced, *Taking Park City*, aired on WTTW Channel 11 in Chicago.

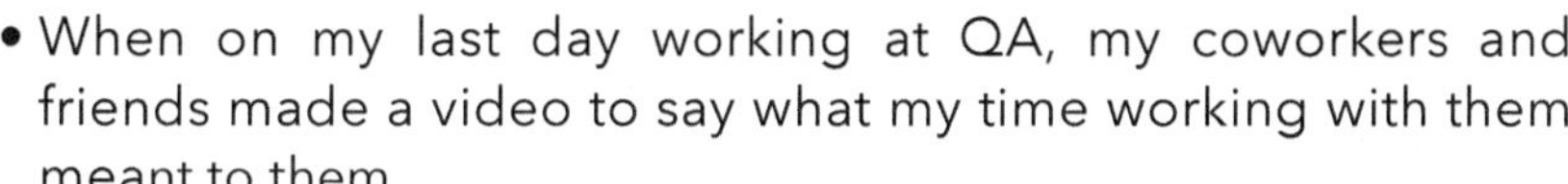

- When on my last day working at QA, my coworkers and friends made a video to say what my time working with them meant to them
- The day my mom called to tell me my father had taken his own life
- When I ran out of gas on the side of a mountain road outside Oakland, bouncing between three freelance jobs and I decided I would write a letter of resignation from who I was–a fixer working for everyone–and become a person with one job and one project to focus on at a time

Each of these steps took me further from who I was. The day my son emerged from his chrysalis was one of the most potent feelings I could ever experience–to be responsible for another person when I'd barely been able to care for myself. Like Arthur, I examined and absorbed every aspect of my life, where I was and what I was meant to become moving forward.

In these moments, I tried to set aside the shock of change and do everything I could to be aware of what I felt, who was there, everything I saw and heard, and even how the air felt. Like Arthur, I woke up each morning expecting nothing, never knowing that my life would change that day. But when the moment came, I always took a deep breath, made the choice I felt ready to make, and stepped into the unknown, because the time was now.

The Quote

MICHAEL CLAYTON: *I'm not the enemy.*
ARTHUR EDENS: *Then who are you?*
MICHAEL CLAYTON: *Don't you know who I am? I'm a fixer.*

The Context

Throughout the story, people constantly ask Michael, "Who are you?" He used to be a lawyer but became very skilled at fixing problems for his firm. However, he's so stuck in that role that even he can't quite identify what he truly believes. He's all go, go, go until an attempt on his life occurs during a moment of contemplation.

Only when he confronts the person who wanted to silence him can he finally say the words that define him: "I'm a fixer." That is all he does. Where he goes from here remains a mystery.

The Lesson

Define yourself. Then redefine yourself.

I am also a fixer. When I saw this movie, I realized that's what I was. I roamed the city, my college campus, and my circle of friends, looking for problems to solve and people to help. And I became really good at it. There wasn't a challenge I couldn't face. I didn't really care about the type of project or work I was doing. I was indifferent to creative pursuits. For me, the thrill was in the fixing.

Moulin Rouge! (2001)

Starring Nicole Kidman, Ewan McGregor, John Leguizamo

The Quotes

CHRISTIAN: *Thank you for curing me of my ridiculous obsession with love.*

CHRISTIAN: *The greatest thing you'll ever learn is just to love and be loved in return.*

The Context

Christian is a penniless writer obsessed with love. He moves to Paris, befriends a group of bohemian artists, accidentally becomes the playwright of a show, and falls in love with Satine, the lead performer at the famous bordello, the Moulin Rouge. Their relationship and its many challenges unfold alongside the play he's writing.

At one point in their story, she is forced to convince him that she doesn't love him, and he breaks down, saying, "Thank you for curing me of my ridiculous obsession with love." But when it's revealed that she truly loves him, the original message of the story returns: "The greatest thing you'll ever learn is just to love and be loved in return."

The Lesson

Let go of the obsession with dreams you can't control ... until they find you.

Since kindergarten I have been obsessed with finding love—that overtly romantic type portrayed in *Moulin Rouge!*. That moment when you lock eyes with someone, the world fades away, and nothing else matters but exploring this other person. Where the main characters are always meant to be together despite the odds, and love wins over all things.

I wanted it so badly that one day I proposed to my crush, who sat in front of me in kindergarten, because I thought that's how you found love. Naturally, she ignored me and my somewhat grown-up request. I'll admit, proposing right before nap time wasn't the best idea, but my heart was in the right place. I saw the beauty in people and the potential we had to be a good match.

Fast forward to high school and the awkward moments of growing up in an urban setting with minimal street smarts. I went to my first homecoming dance dressed in a full suit, inspired by movies from a time when people actually dressed like that for school dances. I walked in, and it was basically a hip-hop dance club. Jeans and T-shirts everywhere. To say I was overdressed is an understatement. Everyone knew me as a nerd and a geek—badges I wore with pride—but this was a different level; I was about to be labeled a leaper.

Thankfully, my resilience kicked in. I hid under the bleachers, took off my suit jacket and the button-up shirt, and just wore a T-shirt. The pants were dark enough not to look like dress pants, and luckily no one noticed I was wearing dress shoes.

When I finally came out, I had the time of my life. I learned how to dance to hip-hop music for the first time. Two of the cool girls actually danced with me, which boosted my confidence. But by the time I was old enough to realize that dancing with me didn't mean they were in love with me, my romantic-obsessed brain had to work hard to accept that point.

In college, my most embarrassing moment related to this was during a first date that included dinner, dancing, and the early stages of intimacy—when I blurted out "I love you." I didn't mean to say it; I was just so caught up in the moment that it slipped out. Instant mood killer. I've always been awkward in this area, but love wasn't in the cards that night.

It took another ten years before I truly experienced romantic love, which eventually led to marriage and parenthood. Aside from that kindergarten moment, my wife, Naomi, is the only person I've ever proposed to. All those awkward attempts at cinematic love added up to a real love I never could have imagined.

Love isn't something you can go out and find, buy, or acquire like a painting. It just happens—like the weather. We have no control over it and must weather the sunshine and storms. When you find it, it's the greatest thing ever. I thank my family for curing me of my ridiculous obsession with what I thought love was, and for loving me the way I was meant to be loved.

Pirates of the Caribbean: At World's End (2007)

Starring Johnny Depp, Orlando Bloom, Keira Knightley, Geoffrey Rush

The Quote

CAPTAIN HECTOR BARBOSSA: *Brace up yards, ya cack-handed deck apes. Dying is the day worth living for!*

The Context

The pirates have all gathered for a showdown with the East India Trading Company. Along the way, every one of them has been both betrayed and a betrayer—victim and aggressor. They continue to fight to escape. Now, they face every foe they've made along the way. On top of it all, it's raining. Oh, and there is a maelstrom forming between them and the enemy.

Elizabeth Swan, who used to dream of being a pirate, has found herself as the new pirate king. She has called on the pirates to stand up and fight! Upon the formation of the maelstrom, she realizes that the only way through is to call on the most experienced pirate to take the helm: her former captor and betrayer, Captain Barbossa. After being betrayed by everyone himself, he steps to the helm

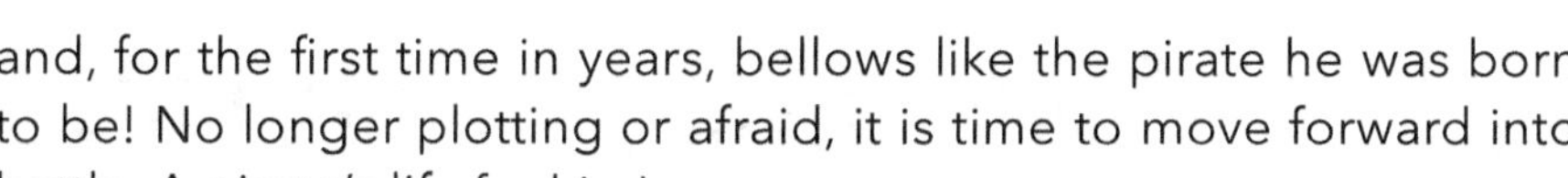

and, for the first time in years, bellows like the pirate he was born to be! No longer plotting or afraid, it is time to move forward into battle. A pirate's life for him!

The Lesson

Be brave and face every day like pirates who've decided to act like fucking pirates!

I love how Captain Barbossa comes to life in this moment! Up until now, he has been concerned only with surviving. Even he said, "Too long my fate has not been in me own hands," right before being betrayed once again. It is at this moment that he takes into his hands his life and the lives of his crew and makes the choice to fight instead of just surviving. He comes alive! Even Elizabeth can't stifle a childlike smile at the sight of a fearsome pirate finally acting like the pirates she used to imagine.

No matter the odds facing you, no matter what isn't working in your favor, it helps to push all of that aside and yell at the top of your lungs. Be unapologetically who you are and do what you came here to do.

I have stood on a set I was managing at the beginning of the day and shouted (in my head), "Brace up yards, ya cack-handed deck apes. Dying is the day worth living for!" It makes the moment more dramatic, the stakes higher, and the journey even more enjoyable. It reminds me to marshal my external resources (my crew) and my internal resources (my spirit) and carry on with the day. One day I will die. And when I do, I will have the memory of each swashbuckling day I have successfully lived to comfort me.

Pirates of the Caribbean: The Curse of the Black Pearl (2003)

Starring Johnny Depp, Orlando Bloom, Keira Knightley

The Quote

CAPTAIN JACK SPARROW: *Me? I'm dishonest, and a dishonest man you can always trust to be dishonest. Honestly. It's the honest ones you want to watch out for, because you can never predict when they're going to do something incredibly … stupid.*

The Context

No one knows which side Jack is on at any given moment. He embodies the very definition of a wild card. His unwilling partner, Will Turner, is so honest that he often ends up doing something stupid in the heat of the moment. In a moment of brilliant eloquence, Jack reveals the truth (from his perspective) about their conflicting personalities.

The Lesson

This is one of those quotes that speaks for itself. I'll let you ruminate on it and find your own meaning. Do you know someone so dishonest that you can trust them to always be dishonest? Do you know someone so honest that you can trust they will always do something stupid?

Remember the Titans (2000)

Starring Denzel Washington, Will Patton, Wood Harris

The Quote

COACH YOAST: *All right, now, I don't want them to gain another yard! You blitz ... all ... night! If they cross the line of scrimmage, I'm gonna take every last one of you out! You make sure they remember, forever, the night they played the Titans! Leave no doubt!*

The Context

Coach Boone has been doing everything he can to bring a fractured football team together. His struggle is about more than winning the games. He is in a fight against racism itself as he works to integrate a Black team and a white team into a cohesive unit with players who trust one another. Assistant Coach Yoast has been hesitant about Boone's tactics while also noticing their benefits along the way. In one of their pivotal games, Yoast finally decides to step up and rally the defense to take a stand.

The Lesson

Do whatever you have to do to achieve your goals!

The first thing that makes this moment special is the voice that speaks it. We have gotten used to Coach Boone's bombastic and demanding tone of voice. It is what has propelled the narrative forward. So, it is surprising when Coach Yoast steps up and demands the best from his players. For the longest time, Yoast was so concerned with taking care of his white players that he wasn't seeing the whole team as something to be nurtured. Boone's style not only brought the team together but also taught Yoast how to look at all the factors at play.

This inspiring moment showed me how to set a goal ("I don't want them to gain another yard"), how hard I should work ("You blitz all night"), and despite all the odds against me, make a clear case for why I belong there ("You make sure they remember forever ...").

I carry that lesson into every project I work on. I focus on the main goal and objective and try not to stop until I have done everything possible to achieve it. Resilience is key to staying in the game. Not every game can be won. Not every project will meet its goals. We can't control every factor of every situation. But we can summon every bit of resilience to stay in the fight long enough to win the moment.

No matter what linebacker or racist umpire stands in your way, you complete your mission.

S1m0ne (2002)

Starring Al Pacino, Catherine Keener, Evan Rachel Wood

The Quote

VIKTOR: *I did it. Tell them they can fry me. I DID IT! It was premeditated! I strangled her … I bludgeoned her … I set her on fire, and then I killed her! I did it!*

The Context

Viktor Taransky is an aging Hollywood director searching for a star. He gets the chance to create a digital star and ends up fooling the entire world into believing she is a real person. When her popularity surpasses his and that of his films, he tries to reveal that she isn't real, but everyone rejects his claim.

When she disappears, he is accused of her murder, which he vigorously denies. When his lawyer offers a ridiculous last-minute defense, Viktor gives up and confesses to her murder, as execution is less painful than what he's currently forced to endure.

The Lesson

Own up to your decisions.

There are times when fighting is not the best approach. It helps to own up to whatever you are accused of. For five years, I managed several event spaces at my college. One crucial part of the job was knowing how to tell people no. I tried my best to be accommo-

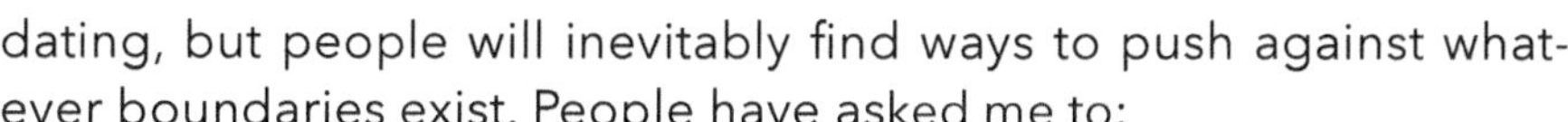

dating, but people will inevitably find ways to push against whatever boundaries exist. People have asked me to:

- Move another person's event because they needed that slot
- Book an event on short notice
- Hold their event even when we had no staff that day
- Make impossible things happen
- Create a Burning Bowl event (my favorite), which involved people writing down things that bothered them and tossing the papers into a fire. It took several conversations to explain that the City of Chicago has strict indoor fire restrictions, and that we could not temporarily disable the fire suppression system for this event.

People want what they want and will go over many hurdles to get it. Many of the people I told no for various reasons would go to my boss to plead their case. When my boss called me into her office, I would immediately ask whether I was fired as a way of breaking the tension—humorous, but also signaling that I owned what I did. Thankfully, my boss always listened to my reasons for being the bearer of bad news. Whether it meant putting extra strain on the staff, ignoring safety protocols, or even changing the flow of time, she supported me. Sometimes she would suggest alternative options to help resolve the situation and keep everyone reasonably happy. By owning the situation, I was given the chance to explain myself and learn whether I had made a mistake.

The Quote

VIKTOR: *I'm not interested in investment and return!
I'm not interested in who pays for anything!
I'm trying to make a movie!*

The Context

The studio head confronts Viktor and explains that his movies aren't making enough money, and his current project has an inflated budget. Viktor, focused only on the art, fires back, "I'm not interested in investment and return! I'm not interested in who pays for anything! I'm trying to make a movie!"

The Lesson

Unfortunately, money is essential.

I have learned the hard way that money turns art into reality. I wish that weren't the case. When I was very young, my parents bought me an illustrated book about where money originates. Its roots are in bartering, but that value was later transferred to paper and coins. I vividly remember approaching my parents and questioning how true this new information was. I thought it was the most ridiculous thing in the world, especially at a time when I was watching cartoons about transforming cars, bears with power emanating from their bellies, and singing chipmunks.

Who determines how valuable each piece of paper is? Why is the stock market full of people betting on the arbitrarily fluctuating prices of goods they cannot see? I truly believed that people should do things for each other out of the goodness of their hearts to keep the world running.

As an adult, I still hold the belief that money should be a less prominent factor in our lives. As a producer, I've accepted that a major part of the job is finding and responsibly using resources, including the budget. Though I may not be skilled at raising money for projects, I excel at using whatever we have to ensure that the people working on the project are well taken care of, and beyond that, that the money makes it onto the screen.

But I've been in countless meetings where I wanted to scream, "I'm not interested in investment and return! I'm not interested in who pays for anything! I'm trying to make a movie!" Alas, that's not how the world works. So I just keep it to myself and continue playing the game.

Serenity (2005)

Starring Nathan Fillion, Alan Tudyk, Gina Torres, Adam Baldwin

The Quote

CAPT. MALCOLM REYNOLDS: *Love. You can learn all the math in the 'Verse, but you take a boat in the air that you don't love, she'll shake you off just as sure as the turning of the worlds. Love keeps her in the air when she oughta fall down, tells you she's hurtin' 'fore she keens. Makes her a home.*

The Context

In the twenty-sixth century, after the Alliance defeats the outer planet Independents, a child genius named River Tam is conditioned into a psychic assassin but escapes with her brother Simon after uncovering government secrets. Hunted by a relentless Alliance operative, the siblings seek refuge aboard the transport spaceship *Serenity*. A battle ensues in which *Serenity* and her crew are victorious over the Alliance. The captain's spaceship has been "tore up plenty." His crew has taken losses. But as they set out for new adventures, he shares a lesson with River: "Love keeps her in the air ..."

The Lesson

No one loves anything quite like Malcolm loves his ship, *Serenity*. It is not just a mode of transportation. It is a part of his crew, his family, and their home all in one. Though they sometimes survive on pure luck, he has also assembled the right people to keep their home afloat in space.

Anything that is part of your journey needs love to keep going. A home can talk to you and tell you what's broken. A company with all the right ingredients can feel like a home and tell you when a part or a person needs replacing or when you need a shoulder to lean on. I love building a team because that group, when aligned and aware of each other, can feel like a ship hurtling through space, ready to take on any challenge.

Whatever structure keeps you going, listen to it. Feel it. Let it tell you when it needs help. Don't take it for granted. And above all, love it. If you do, it will keep you alive and in the air.

The Quote

JAYNE COBB: *She is starting to damage my calm.*

The Context

The crew of the *Serenity* has just landed on a mysterious planet where everyone who lived there died long ago. As they piece together what happened, one of the crew, River, begins crying and shouting. She somehow feels the presence of the dead all over the planet.

Her unpredictable behavior in an already creepy situation causes strongman Jayne to say, "She is starting to damage my calm."

The Lesson

Recognize when your calm is being damaged.

There are many different types of people. Some of them can stay calm and encourage calmness in any situation they face. I have been told I possess that ability. Then there are those who, through no fault of their own (or perhaps all their fault), damage the calm of everyone around them. To me, it often feels like a relentless wave of worry.

Instead of worrying about their anxiety, I've learned to pause and recognize when the person I am dealing with in the moment is "starting to damage my calm." By naming it, I can take steps to manage my own reactions, deescalate the situation, and address the underlying cause. I will do what I can to bring peace to the worrier, but ultimately I have to accept that their calm is their responsibility to manage. The same goes for my own calm. And that is how we begin to repair the damage.

Shaft (2000)

Starring Samuel L. Jackson, Vanessa Williams, Christian Bale

The Quote

JOHN SHAFT: *Too black for the uniform, too blue for the brothers.*

The Context

Shaft is the godfather of rizz, a smooth-talking ladies' man and officer of the law who always comes out on top. Right now, he's angry because both sides of his identity refuse to accept him.

The Lesson

Living in duality is challenging.

Black men have a history of being harassed, or worse, by the police. The police have a history of over-policing the Black community. So imagine what it's like being a Black man upholding the law—trying to serve and protect, while being viewed as an enemy by the very people you are trying to help. At the same time, your colleagues may see you as "less than" them.

I've faced multiple dualities in my life. Since birth, I've always been an old soul in a young body. In elementary school, I was called an "Oreo" because I was Black on the outside and white on the inside, based on how I "acted white." In high school, I empathized with teachers and fellow students alike. Whether someone was a nerd, jock, Asian, or in a band, I always made time to sit with them and learn more about their "thing." In college, I became a bridge between faculty and students in our film and video practicum. In my career, I make it a point to know everyone I work with or alongside—from security guards to CEOs—equally.

We all seek community in some form. Some find "their" community and thrive within it for a lifetime. I, on the other hand, find solace jumping from one community to another. While I lack roots, I gain a wealth of diverse experiences. Some have rejected me because I didn't fully belong, but others welcomed me and showed me what makes their perspective special.

While it's important to recognize how you do and don't belong to certain groups, it's more crucial to accept yourself as you are. Don't seek approval from the badge you're "too Black" for or from the brother you're "too blue" for. Just be yourself and enjoy your complicated journey.

Sherlock Holmes (2009)

Starring Robert Downey Jr., Jude Law, Rachel McAdams

The Quote

SHERLOCK HOLMES: *My mind rebels at stagnation! Give me problems! Give me work!*

The Context

Sherlock Holmes does not do well with boredom.

The Lesson

Embrace both the busyness and the stagnation.

I spent the first thirty years of my life doing everything I could to fill my time. If I wasn't working, creating, or collaborating, I would mentally berate myself. If I didn't have a problem to solve, I would roam the school halls looking for problems to solve, like Batman roams the streets for evildoers.

Most of this stems from feelings from my childhood home. I did not want to be there. It was my prison and the place where most of my bad memories were born. So I dedicated myself to joining multiple clubs, inserting myself into people's lives, and staying active as much as I could.

The upside is that I did a lot of good for other people and made friends. The downside is that I began to attach my self-worth to the only role I thought I was worthy of playing: fixer. If I was fixing some-

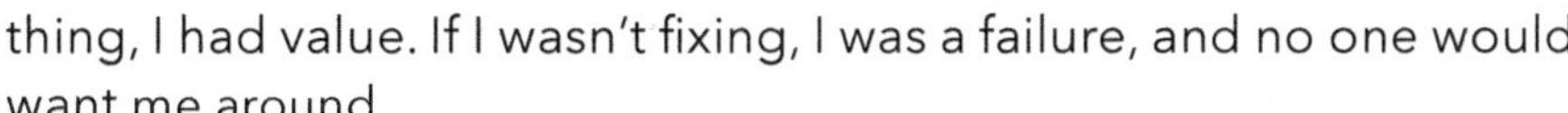

thing, I had value. If I wasn't fixing, I was a failure, and no one would want me around.

It wasn't until my forties that I realized I have value no matter what. While it is important and help others, it is equally important to be of service to ourselves–to solve our own problems or just allow ourselves empty, unstructured periods to enjoy our time on this planet or rejuvenate.

Stagnation will happen regardless of how busy we are. It helps to allow those moments of emptiness to occur. We may learn more about ourselves than we can when constantly active. The key is balance.

The Quote

SHERLOCK HOLMES: *My journey took me somewhat further down the rabbit hole than I intended, and though I dirtied my fluffy white tail, I have emerged, enlightened.*

The Context

Sherlock is in the middle of a tough case. He has a mountain of clues, but cannot figure out how they are all connected. He is faced with a cult of religious fanatics who have rituals he does not believe in. After a monumental setback, he turns to his usual meditation to find the answer. When that fails, he realizes the only way to find the connection is to lose himself in the very ritual his rival inspires, with a touch of a drug normally used for eye surgery.

What ensues is a nightmarish hallucination that brings him closer to the solution, which he reveals the following day. He describes his journey as such.

The Lesson

It can be a challenging journey to reach a calm destination.

Life can be messy. Sometimes calm meditation can provide the answers we're seeking. Emptying the mind and soothing the soul can help us focus. However, life is rarely calm and peaceful. There are times when chaos and immersion, even if uncomfortable, can help us find solutions to our problems.

Let me be clear: I am not advocating drug use (especially misuse of eye surgery solutions) to solve your issues. But sitting with a problem can be an effective way to find a path forward. It can be as simple and insightful as talking to a friend in a safe environment where you can honestly share your feelings. Acknowledging these feelings instead of suppressing them allows healing.

Other activities that can help on this journey include visiting rage rooms, hitting a ball, riding a roller coaster, or going to a rave. These experiences and more can serve as ways to navigate your emotions and arrive at a place where you can see clearly and choose your next step.

The Sum of All Fears (2002)

Starring Ben Affleck, Morgan Freeman, Liev Schreiber

The Quote

BILL CABOT: *What's the T-shirt say?*
DEPOT WORKER: *I am a bomb technician. If you see me running, try to catch up.*

The Context

White House official Bill Cabot is touring a Russian nuclear facility. During the tour, he notices a worker wearing a T-shirt with Russian writing. When he asks for a translation, he's told it says, "I am a bomb technician. If you see me running, try to catch up."

The Lesson

I've always considered myself adventurous and mostly fearless. I even cured my fear of spiders by forcing myself to watch the movie *Arachnophobia*—a bold but surprisingly effective strategy. But one fear has clung to me: swimming in deep water where I can't touch the bottom. Whenever I wade too far into the ocean, a flicker of irrational worry rises that something unseen might brush past me. As soon as I can stand again, calm returns.

That fear resurfaced in Barcelona one freezing January morning when I tried scuba diving for the first time. My instructor was an experienced diver offering lessons through Airbnb, and my excitement easily outweighed my nerves—at least until the cold water hit and I began my descent. The moment the murky depths surrounded me, panic crept in. My heart raced with thoughts of unseen danger until I caught sight of my guide, moving calmly through the water as if strolling down a sidewalk.

Watching his ease, I remembered the saying, "I'm a bomb technician. If you see me running, try to keep up." My fear dissolved as I realized I could trust his calm to guide my own. The rest of the dive was pure wonders especially when he suddenly removed his fins and danced atop an old SUV resting on the sea floor. Only later did I learn it was a training site for navy divers. That surreal moment cemented a lesson I carry everywhere: When you're out of your depth—literally or figuratively—trust the people who know more than you.

The Quote

JACK RYAN: *Cabot did tell me he had a source in Russia.*
ANATOLI GRUSHKOV: *To keep the back channels open.*
JACK RYAN: *In hopes of staving off disaster.*

The Context

Jack Ryan's mentor, Cabot, has been texting with a secret contact for years. No one, not even Cabot, knew who he was—only that he was a trustworthy source in Russia. Cabot is gravely injured in a terrorist attack. Before he dies, he offers this contact to Jack so he can gather information and stop an escalating conflict between the United States and Russia.

At the end of the story, the contact reveals himself to Jack as one of the Russian president's top advisors. Despite official communication between their respective presidents and governments, Anatoli and Cabot kept the back channels of communication open in the hope of preventing disaster. Jack is now the beneficiary of that back channel.

The Lesson

I've always believed in the importance of rules and official procedures. They exist for a reason. But sometimes the "right" channels move too slowly to solve an urgent problem. That's when back channels–those informal, human connections outside the hierarchy–become essential. A quick conversation with the right security guard or staff member can save hours of red tape and make the impossible suddenly possible.

I learned this lesson from my boss and mentor, Kari, who treated everyone–from department heads to janitors–with equal respect. Together, we ran the college's end-of-year celebration, which required meticulous coordination, including clearing a parking lot for a massive tent setup. Despite posting warning signs and following every procedure, we arrived at 4 a.m. to find twenty cars still parked there, and the official channels were useless.

That's when Kari's back channel saved us. She convinced the delivery crew to lend us furniture dollies and muscle power, and together we manually rolled eleven cars out of the way before dawn. The rest were towed or claimed by sleepy owners in robes. The event went off flawlessly because Kari understood that while rules keep order, relationships get results. Ever since, I've made a habit of cultivating those behind-the-scenes connections that make magic happen when it matters most.

Terminator 3: Rise of the Machines (2003)

Starring Arnold Schwarzenegger, Nick Stahl, Claire Danes

The Quote

TERMINATOR: *Desire is irrelevant. I am a machine.*

The Context

The Terminator (model T-101) is a machine sent back in time and programmed to protect John Connor, the future leader of the human resistance. Another Terminator (model T-X) was also sent back to kill John. The T-X gains the advantage and reprograms the T-101 to also kill him.

When the T-101 and John come face-to-face, John reminds it of its original mission to protect him. The T-101 becomes conflicted. Does it fail in its initial mission, or follow its current programming? When John reminds the T-101 of its mission, it coldly responds, "Desire is irrelevant. I am a machine."

The Lesson

Desire is relevant. I am not a machine.

As a twentysomething who didn't grow up with many social skills, I spent a lot of time wondering what was wrong with me. When things didn't go my way in dating, I analyzed the situation and kept working on myself. When dating goes wrong and "ghosting" occurs (a term we didn't have in the early 2000s), it's nearly impossible to find healthy closure.

I justified my lack of social awareness by thinking I might just be a machine. If I were a machine, then anything I desired wasn't meant to be, and I just had to accept that and continue with my mission. I believed that helping people would give me the comfort I longed for. I thought that being a good person would lead to the love I wanted. I thought that if people rejected me, then it was meant to be because my desires weren't relevant.

Over time I realized I am not a machine. I am very much human. I am also responsible for my actions and can pursue what I desire because, as a human, my desires matter to me. I understand that my desires matter only to me and the people who truly care about me. I also realize I won't always get what I want, but I should be open to what comes my way. Lastly, I understand that just because someone else's desires don't match my own, it doesn't mean my desires are any less relevant.

Training Day (2001)

Starring Denzel Washington, Ethan Hawke

The Quote

ALONZO HARRIS: *You know I'm surgical with this bitch, Jake.*

The Context

Alonzo is a corrupt cop chasing his more principled younger partner, Jake, with a shotgun, which he is very skilled at using. While Jake is cornered, Alonzo constantly taunts him.

The Lesson

This line works in all situations.

- When you're cooking on the stove: "You know I'm surgical with this bitch, Jake."
- When you're driving with precision: "You know I'm surgical with this bitch, Jake."
- When you're operating a crane: "You know I'm surgical with this bitch, Jake."
- When you're making a spreadsheet: "You know I'm surgical with this bitch, Jake."
- When you're playing with light sabers: "You know I'm surgical with this bitch, Jake."
- When you're playing an instrument: "You know I'm surgical with this bitch, Jake."

- When you're vacuuming: "You know I'm surgical with this bitch, Jake."
- When you're gardening: "You know I'm surgical with this bitch, Jake."
- When you're making love: "You know I'm surgical with this bitch, Jake."

Bonus points if the person you're talking to is named Jake!

Three Couples (2004)

Starring Mary Dehne, Bill Hainsworth, Ivan Ortega, River Ozgur, Lauren Ryland, Jenni Sumerak

The Quote

HANK: *Stop thinking so hard and just have some fun, will ya?*

The Context

Hank is taking a break from anniversary sex with one of his roommates. His wife gave him permission for this activity. When he suggests his wife join them, she hesitates, to which he sharply replies, "Stop thinking so hard and just have some fun, will ya?"

The Lesson

This is an anthem against overthinking.

I am a strategist at heart. I won chess championships early on. From a young age I had a knack for moving people like chess pieces around a situation. By my mid-twenties I was so wound up from years of trying to orchestrate every moment that I forgot to enjoy them. I was so focused on the future that I didn't appreciate the present. I was thinking so hard about what to do next that I lost sight of the achievements I already had.

This quote is from one of many films my friend Brian McQuery wrote and directed. We were having fun in a penthouse apartment with a large crew and a cast of six. When the actor playing Hank said that line, I nearly did a spit take. As one of the producers, I knew the script inside out. But his delivery was just right, and I took it to heart. Being the editor too, I watched it repeatedly and fought to ensure that take was the one we used. It felt genuine, playful, and full of masculine sass.

I've spent the last three years finally letting go of constant planning and strategizing. I'll never completely stop, and I don't want to. But I like having a plan and not overthinking it—just having fun with whatever happens. It takes constant effort and reminders, and this quote always comes to mind at the right moment to do just that.

V for Vendetta (2005)

Starring Natalie Portman, Hugo Weaving, Stephen Rea

The Quote

FINCH: *I suddenly had this feeling that everything was connected. It's like I could see the whole thing, one long chain of events that stretched all the way back before Larkhill. I felt like I could see everything that happened, and everything that is going to happen. It was like a perfect pattern, laid out in front of me. And I realized we're all part of it, and all trapped by it.*

The Context

A masked man named V threatens to blow up Parliament in an effort to shake the public out of apathy and stand against the corrupt government. Detective Finch is trying to stop it and understand V's motivations. He visits the site of a mass disaster from the city's recent past and suspects there is a connection he hasn't uncovered yet. In his own words, "It's just a feeling."

The Lesson

I see patterns everywhere. I am sensitive to the connections between things, people, and history. I can tell you every event and moment that led to the creation of a project or the evolution of a romantic relationship. One of the things that has aided me in my producing journey is the ability to read all of the cast and crew in the room. I know roughly how they are feeling when they enter, how they are collaborating throughout the day, what information they have heard, and what they missed. Through my interaction with people, I can see patterns in their behavior and have a pretty good idea of what stimuli will encourage and discourage them.

We had an audio guy who would always light up when I brought him an almond croissant in the morning during the daily breakfast run. But I started to notice him hovering around the pastry table after lunch, as if he were looking for another croissant for a late snack. He would be sad if one wasn't there, so I secretly ordered two. One for the morning on his desk, and the second I would hide by my monitor. After lunch, I would sneak the second one onto his desk when he wasn't looking. This small gesture helped him get through the day. By being receptive to his patterns, I was able to give him an enjoyable experience, with the reward being his consistent effort and communication.

On a larger scale, I have worked for several organizations and companies where I could detail the domino effect of events that led to their eventual downfall or success. I may not have had every detail, but I could paint an accurate picture that others could fill in to complete the story.

We are all connected in an endless evolution of cause and effect. It's when we are receptive to those patterns that we can do our best not to be surprised by future developments. I never judge a pattern. I just observe and note the patterns that emerge. Sometimes I play a game and try to guess the next move that will naturally occur. I don't act on the prediction; I just keep it to myself. If I am right, I do an internal emotional happy dance. If I am wrong, I learn from what I might have missed and move on.

Seeing patterns is a hard sensation for me to turn off. Over time, I have learned how to control my reactions to those patterns and use my power strategically. No matter your sensitivity, do your best to be open to the serendipitous nature of life.

2010s to Now

Agents of S.H.I.E.L.D. (2013-2020)

Season 5, Episode 22: The End

Starring Clark Gregg, Ming-Na Wen, Chloe Bennet, Iain De Caestecker

The Quote

PHIL COULSON: *I've given you all the tools you need to handle this. Now you find the strength in your heart to appeal to his good nature, and if you can't, find the strength in your arms to beat his ass senseless. We're out of time. Go.*

The Context

S.H.I.E.L.D. Director Phil Coulson and Agent Daisy Johnson have evolved from a boss/employee relationship to mentor/mentee, and now to something akin to a father/daughter connection. Coulson always has a plan and a way to bring out the best in people. Daisy trusts him more than anyone else and will always charge in to save her "family." Now they are facing an extremely powerful friend turned foe, with the literal fate of the world in the balance.

Phil reveals that he is not going to join her on the battlefield for the first time in their journey together. He is dying and can barely stand. Livid, she points out that it is his job to reason with people and help them see a better path than violence. With his last bit of strength, he stands and reminds her that she has everything she needs to save the world from destruction on her own, whether she realizes it or not. S.H.I.E.L.D.'s mission is to save lives. But if she cannot save his life, then she must take it to save the world.

The Lesson

This is the true meaning of parenthood. When Phil and Daisy's relationship began, Daisy was young and inexperienced. There was mistrust on both sides, but mutual respect grew into shared love. He took responsibility for her training and development, and she trusted him more and more. He was always there to lead, and she was a loyal soldier. As he grew older, it became clearer that he might not always be around, but she refused to accept that idea. Now they faced a crossroads where she had to go out on her own and do what he has been training her to do all along: trust herself to live in this world without him.

From Daisy's perspective, it's hard to imagine that world. Phil is all she has known in this important chapter of her life. He is the man with the plan, a man they can always trust to help them succeed. She is used to being a weapon that, when given directions, can handle almost anything. But now she must use her brain, her strength, and the heart she didn't realize she had all along to do what he used to do.

Going out on your own and facing unknown situations can be scary, but destiny won't let that fear keep you in place forever. We all have to face a world without the person who raised us. It's inevitable.

That is the circle of life and the circle of mentorship. Each generation prepares the next to prepare the next. We all have the tools we need in our moment of calling. We just have to trust ourselves and take the next step.

Andor (2022)

Season 1, Episode 6: The Eye

Season 2, Episode 5: I Have Friends Everywhere

Starring Diego Luna, Stellan Skarsgård, Adria Arjona, Genevieve O'Reilly, Forest Whitaker, Alex Lawther

The Quote

NEMIK: *Climb. Full climb now!*

CASSIAN: *What did you give him? I'm pegged here. I don't have the speed to make it. And now you want me to climb?*

NEMIK: *Climb!*

The Context

Andor follows thief-turned-rebel Cassian Andor as he becomes radicalized and drawn into the early formation of the Rebel Alliance in the years leading up to *Rogue One*, the Star Wars film depicting the desperate mission to steal the Death Star plans. Our heroes have just robbed an Imperial bank vault and are trying desperately to escape in large spacecraft designed for hauling, not for speed. They have had very little time to get to know one another, let alone trust each other. But they must press on together. In the midst of the daring escape through a dazzling meteor shower called "The Eye," their navigator, Nemik, is injured, and the pilot, Andor, is flying blind. Their quiet debates about why they joined the rebellion have now reached a climax in a moment where disbelief turns into trust.

With every bit of strength Nemik has left, he screams his navigation instructions to Andor at the top of his lungs. Andor is in disbelief because they are surrounded by danger. With one heavy, gasping breath, Nemik yells, "Climb!" in a way that says, "Trust me, please!"

The Lesson

Despite everything going wrong around us, despite what you see and hear, and despite what you've been trained to believe, you need to trust your leader and your team.

This is one of the most powerful scenes I have ever experienced in any cinematic universe. It is visually stunning, like a multicolored meteor shower that is also deadly. The cinematography and acting effectively convey the danger the characters face, and we understand that the stakes for this mission are extremely high.

Andor was right to question Nemik's strange directions. They were flying a large, low-maneuverability ship amid flying objects that could kill them, chased by enemy fighters. The last place they should go is up into the storm. But Nemik had an old piece of tech that could map the storm and find the safest path out.

In 1965, Bruce Tuckman developed a model for team development that describes the stages it goes through: forming (when the team forms but is unsure of each other's roles), storming (when roles are established but conflicts arise), norming (when trust begins to form), and performing (where the team works efficiently together).

Andor and Nemik's team came together over several months, with Andor joining only days before this mission. They knew each other's skills and roles but not their backgrounds or motivations. They experienced conflict early on, believing they had a plan and rehearsing it, yet still harboring distrust, and some were not confident in themselves. During the heist, they moved into norming as they faced one challenge after another, staying together and adjusting to unpredictable issues.

I believe the moment Nemik yells "Climb!" and Andor pauses to decide to let go of past issues and trust his teammate is when they finally perform. There was trust that each person would cover their part and do everything possible to survive and succeed. Each of us holds a piece of the puzzle, and trust is what makes those pieces fit and stay together.

As a producer I've been in countless situations where, logically, success seemed impossible. There's never enough time, money, resources, or people, and everyone knows it. Often, all hope feels lost. Even worse, we waste what little time we have talking about how little time is left.

In those moments, I've been fortunate that someone would shout "Climb!" Sometimes it was me saying, "We can do this. Let's figure out the next step," or "How can we change the plan and still hit our goal?" Other times, someone else would suggest, "Let's do X," or "What if we try Y?" Despite the odds, we held onto hope that a solution existed and quickly gained everyone's trust that we had a plan and the means to survive.

When building your team, seek not only skilled and capable people but also those who hold onto hope—those who see things unconventionally and inspire trust in others. These qualities are hard to spot on a résumé, but you'll recognize them in certain people.

The Quote

SAW: *We're the rhydo, kid. We're the fuel. We're the thing that explodes when there's too much friction in the air. Let it in, boy. That's freedom calling. Let it in. Let it run. Let it run wild!*

The Context

Saw Gerrera is the leader of an extreme faction fighting for freedom within the evolving rebellion. He hovers over a younger rebel named Wilmon who is carefully stealing a dangerous substance essential to their cause. Unlike Saw, Wilmon wears a mask because the substance is toxic. Saw, accustomed to the toxin, breathes it in and uses this moment of madness to inspire Wilmon to remove his mask and inhale the toxins freely.

Saw explains that they, the forgotten and unloved freedom fighters, are the fuel of the rebellion. It's a masterful example of how to turn a young, skilled mind into that of an extremist.

The Lesson

Let your passion run wild.

Saw's moving speech can be used to inspire those in any situation. It stirs the soul and focuses the resolve. It also pushes a person to let go and let their spirit run wild. While I don't condone Saw's brand of extremism, which is tantamount to terrorism, we all need inspiration to make it through the combustible moments we face. Passion is hard to find. When you truly find something you are passionate about, fuel it in every way you can and run with it until it's done.

My passion for films is what has fueled me throughout my life and has then translated to exploring them in this book. Motivational quotes have always fueled the self-help industry. But movie quotes benefit from following the characters they inspire as they try to achieve their own goals. They also invite examination into how those moments affect our real lives.

Whatever positively fuels you, let it in!

Avengers: Infinity War (2018)

Starring Robert Downey Jr., Chris Hemsworth, Chris Evans, Josh Brolin

The Quote

TONY STARK: *Don't, don't. Don't engage. We almost got this off!*

The Context

Thanos is on a mission to destroy half of all life in the universe using a gauntlet containing powerful stones. Members of the Avengers and the Guardians of the Galaxy have concocted a plan to stop him: get the gauntlet off his hand.

The plan nearly works. They restrain him and struggle to get the gauntlet off. Star-Lord, one of the Guardians, asks Thanos a question, the answer to which angers him. Tony, who is working to get the gauntlet off, realizes Star-Lord's anger could jeopardize the entire plan, so he yells, "Don't, don't. Don't engage. We almost got this off!" Star-Lord doesn't listen and beats up Thanos, which causes the group to lose their respective grips on Thanos before the gauntlet is removed.

The Lesson

Know when to engage and when to wait.

Parenthood is one of the hardest tests of patience. When I became a parent, I received the best advice from a friend: "Your child is not giving you a hard time; they are just having a hard time." It is a tough lesson to remember when poo-filled diapers are being flung at your head or a hangry meltdown is forcing you to evacuate a museum as quickly as possible. Parenthood is tough.

It took me years to realize that my anger and reaction to my child's distress made the problem worse. When difficult moments occur, our reaction can be more harmful than helpful. Don't get me wrong. I kept my cool plenty of times. But every once in a while, I would break and yell for him to stop banging on the table or throwing things. It is only recently that I have learned better when to do nothing and when it is time to engage.

If he is threatening his life, engage. If he is able to knock over a glass, engage. If he is throwing Uno cards around the room, no need to engage. He is dealing with his anger in the way he feels he needs to. Cards can be picked up later. But egos can get in the way of the process, and any chaos or disorganization can trigger a negative response. Take a breath, think about why this moment is taking place, and ask yourself, do I need to engage, and if I do, will it make the problem worse?

This dynamic occurs in parenting, work, and all throughout life. We don't always have to engage with every slight we perceive. It takes just as much strength to practice restraint as it does to jump in and try to be a hero. Or inflict pain in revenge for pain caused. Star-Lord put the entire universe in jeopardy because he could not wait for the right time to engage.

Black Panther (2018)

Starring Chadwick Boseman, Michael B. Jordan, Lupita Nyong'o, Danai Gurira, Angela Bassett, John Kani

The Quotes

QUEEN RAMONDA: *Show him who you are!*

KING T'CHAKA: *Stand up! You are a king!*

The Context

The King of Wakanda has died. His son, Prince T'Challa, is fighting his chief rival, M'Baku, in ritualistic combat to become the next king. M'Baku manages to gain the upper hand. T'Challa looks over to his mother, Queen Ramonda, who screams, "Show him who you are!" T'Challa rises and does just that. He defeats M'Baku and shows mercy at the same time.

After completing the challenge, he takes part in the next ritual, which involves visiting the astral plane and meeting his late father, King T'Chaka, once more. In a heartfelt moment, the son bows again to his father out of instinct and respect. The father, in a stern

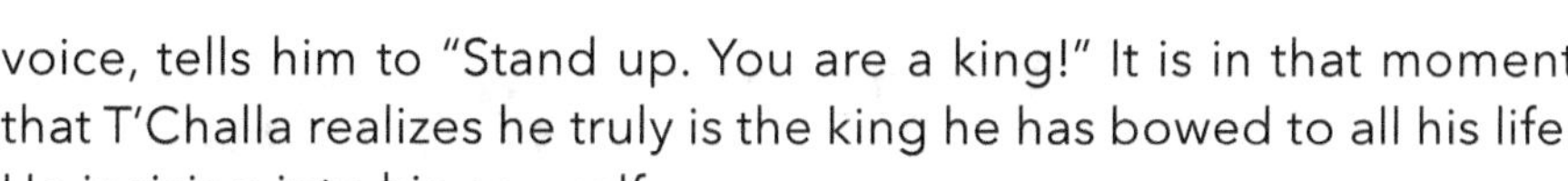

voice, tells him to "Stand up. You are a king!" It is in that moment that T'Challa realizes he truly is the king he has bowed to all his life. He is rising into his new self.

The Lesson

Show the world (and yourself) who you are.

We are all trying to be or do something. There is a distant goal we aim to reach, another version of ourselves we want to become. We think that one day things will be better if only we had X amount of money or attention. My desire has always been to find a true, deep relationship.

We focus so much on what is missing from our lives and how much better it would be if we got that thing, that we ignore the whole person we are now. We have everything we need to live in the present moment. Until our dying day, we can boast that we have survived every day of our lives. No matter how happy or sad, enlightened or debilitating those days were, we made it. And we have the skills and emotional scars to prove it.

When faced with a fresh situation or a new group of people, I remind myself to show them who I am: I remind myself to be my whole and true self. I have worth and several skills to offer anyone willing to accept them. I remind myself that I have brought comfort to thousands of people and will continue to do so. I remind myself that I have nothing to prove, only to be who I am, and that is enough to face any situation.

When I get knocked down, make a mistake, or unintentionally hurt someone (because those things will happen), I also remind myself, "Stand up. I am a producer or stand up. I am a parent." Though I am not a producer in Hollywood working with multimillion-dollar budgets or commanding thousands of crew members, I am still a producer. I am the producer I was meant to be in this moment. Nothing can take away the progress I have made or the person I will become. I choose not to judge myself for the person I have not yet become because I have no idea whether that person will ever exist.

I choose to honor the person I am. I choose to show the world who I am. And I choose to show myself that I am enough.

Captain America: The Winter Soldier (2014)

Starring Chris Evans, Samuel L. Jackson, Scarlett Johansson, Sebastian Stan

The Quote

NICK FURY: *This man declined the Nobel Peace Prize. He said that peace is not an achievement but a responsibility. It's stuff like this that gives me trust issues.*

The Context

Nick Fury, director of the spy agency S.H.I.E.L.D., has just been betrayed by his longtime friend. He can count how many people he trusts on one hand, and he just lost another one. He isn't even shocked, as he already had trust issues, but now he is justified.

The Lesson

All we can do is open ourselves enough not to lose ourselves to other people's choices.

There aren't enough hands to count the reasons I have trust issues. People are complicated and often clash with our expectations. They not only lie to those around them but also to themselves.

I am an optimist with trust issues. I hope for the best in people—that they'll come through, speak their minds, and support me. But I also prepare for the worst—that they might not even know what the truth is. I find no pleasure in being proved right that people can be untrustworthy.

When I face those tough moments, I repeat, "It's stuff like this that gives me trust issues," to remind myself that being cautious is natural and that I will move on from this as I always do.

My best friend Chris taught me that I kept myself guarded because I was afraid people would leave me (like my mother left my father, justified though she was) or try to destroy me (like my father did by making me be what he wanted). It was then that I realized that people aren't inherently evil; rather, their choices can unintentionally clash with my expectations.

Creed (2015)

Starring Michael B. Jordan, Sylvester Stallone, Tessa Thompson

The Quote

ROCKY BALBOA: *One step at a time. One punch at a time. One round at a time.*

The Context

Rocky Balboa is coaching young Adonis Creed (born Adonis Johnson) for his upcoming fight against the heavyweight champion of the world. Creed is the clear underdog but has the determination to go all the way and the skill of a legendary underdog in his corner. During intense training, Rocky yells to Creed, "One step at a time. One punch at a time. One round at a time."

The Lesson

No, I am not an advocate of boxing. I've never punched anyone in my life. So I decided to modify this quote to fit my perspective.

One step at a time.

One choice at a time.

One day at a time.

We can only ever take the next step, whether physically or emotionally. No matter how much we worry, we can only make the next choice available to us. We can only live in one day. The goal is to take the next step that leads us to the next choice and gets us to the end of the day, and then repeat.

The bigger picture is an illusion. Goals are important, but each step we take, every choice we make, and each day we live will guide us not to where we want to go but to where we are meant to be. Accept the journey as it unfolds before you.

The Quote

ADONIS CREED: *I have to prove it!*
ROCKY BALBOA: *Prove what?*
ADONIS CREED: *That I'm not a mistake!*

The Context

Adonis Creed was born from an affair. After his father, Apollo Creed, died, his wife took Adonis in and raised him as her own. He is now fighting the heavyweight champion of the world. Up until this fight, he has managed to keep his father's identity a secret. But now, he's fighting while wearing his father's name and colors.

The match is brutal. As his trainer, Rocky Balboa, shows concern for Adonis before the final round, Adonis pleads with him not to stop the fight. He wants to prove he is not a mistake.

The Lesson

We all struggle to prove we belong in this life.

I don't know the endless possibilities that came together to bring me here. All I know is that I am here. I exist. I know people who know me and acknowledge that I exist. Right now, I am typing words on a digital page for you to read. My existence has been proven.

But like you, I still feel the daily urge to find out why I exist and to leave a mark on this world and in the minds of those I meet. Every day at work, every creative project, every mission I complete, and every interaction with friends and family is another chance to prove I did well in this life. In our quest for relevance, it's all too easy to forget that we have nothing left to prove. We are here. We've done what we can in every situation we've faced.

Celebrate the you that exists in the present moment. It's okay to strive for more–to do better–for what's ahead. But don't be too hard on yourself for not living up to the high expectations you've set. You exist. You are not a mistake. Even if, like Creed, you exist because of a lapse in your parents' judgment involving money, you still exist. You were meant to be here. And you have nothing to prove.

Creed II (2018)

Starring Michael B. Jordan, Sylvester Stallone, Tessa Thompson

The Quote

ROCKY BALBOA: *If you want to change things in a big way, then you gotta make some big changes.*

The Context

Boxing champ Adonis Creed has been knocked down and is trying to get up again. As he considers returning to the ring, his trainer, Rocky Balboa, encourages him to make big changes to how and where he trains for his next fight.

The Lesson

Don't be stagnant, my friends.

There are countless things to explore in this world–places, activities, adventures. Sometimes, we get bogged down in our daily routines, making it hard to break free and try something new. Adulting can feel like one long, never-ending to-do list. Parenting is about keeping a little person alive and entertained, one day at a time. Our jobs are literal to-do lists that we're constantly judged on, one task at a time.

We live life in small increments, and change can be difficult to implement step by step. Sometimes, you have to make big changes and see where they lead. Toss the game board into the air and start fresh, or move the pieces into new positions. Change jobs. Move to a different country. Try a new cuisine. Say yes to the crazy trip your friend suggests.

If you love your life as it is, that's wonderful. I'm so happy for you and a little envious. But everyone wishes something were different about their life. If all you need is to buy that one thing from that one store to truly fix everything, go do it. But if you're stuck in a routine where your life's structure doesn't quite feel right, I would take a big, deliberate leap to change your course.

I love planning ahead. My online calendar is always up to date. My nickname at work is Callsheet–the document sent out before a shoot day with all the details. And like the starship *Enterprise*, I often plot a course and follow it. But every once in a while, while riding the bus to my destination, I like to hop off early and explore the area in which I've unexpectedly found myself. This simple act completely shifts my planned route and invites a whole new adventure.

I'm not saying you should abandon your children or leave your construction job while the big metal beam swings overhead. If you have responsibilities, don't ignore them. Any change I make, big or small, is always considered in light of how it will affect my son. But my son's presence won't keep me stuck in a job or place that's not fulfilling. Writing this book was a significant change for me. I'm so glad I made that choice, and I'm even happier you chose to read it.

Creed III (2023)

Starring Michael B. Jordan, Tessa Thompson, Wood Harris

The Quote

TONY "LITTLE DUKE" EVERS JR.: *Let go of the fear! Let go of the guilt. Let go of whatever was, and walk into what is.*

The Context

Boxing legend Adonis Creed is in the final round of his toughest fight yet against a former friend and fierce rival. But the hardest battle is the one he fights within himself. His coach, Little Duke, gives him one last pep talk, encouraging him to change his mindset because he needs to "stop boxing and start fighting." Creed is holding onto a lot of pain and mistakes from the past. To win this battle, he must let go of the past and focus on what is now.

The Lesson

Let go and take the next step.

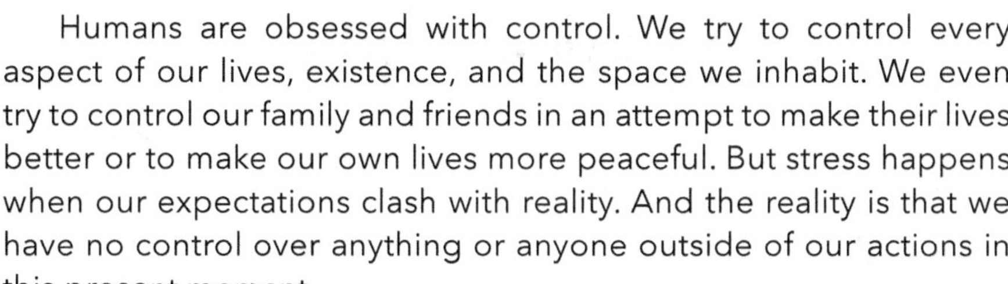

Humans are obsessed with control. We try to control every aspect of our lives, existence, and the space we inhabit. We even try to control our family and friends in an attempt to make their lives better or to make our own lives more peaceful. But stress happens when our expectations clash with reality. And the reality is that we have no control over anything or anyone outside of our actions in this present moment.

Creed carries a lot of pain from his past. He has spent his career trying to prove he's not a mistake, to show he can live up to his father's name, and to cement his own legacy. His former coach, Rocky Balboa, faced a similar barrier, as he was perpetually afraid of losing everything. Those fears are a heavy burden and serve no purpose other than to distract us from what we can do right here and now.

I like that this quote uses walking as a metaphor for change. Every time we take a step—literally or figuratively—we move from one place to the next and from one experience to the next. We might see or hear things differently as we walk. The next step takes us further away from who we were and closer to who we will become. But we can take only one step at a time.

As I said before, the lessons of the past can either guide us or trap us. And in crucial moments, it helps to let everything go, put down all emotional baggage, and trust that the next step will be the right one. We can learn from the past and prepare for the future, but sometimes those memories and hopes can distract us from the present moment.

Da 5 Bloods (2020)

Starring Delroy Lindo, Jonathan Majors, Clarke Peters, Chadwick Boseman

The Quote

STAFF SGT. STORMIN' NORMAN: *You're talking about Dr. King. You're talking about a man of peace. I'm as mad as everybody. All us Bloods got a right to be, but we Bloods won't let nobody use our rage against us. We control our rage.*

The Context

An African American military unit led by Stormin' Norman is deep in the jungles of Vietnam during the war. They are enraged to learn that Dr. Martin Luther King Jr. has just been assassinated. While the rest of Norman's team wants to turn their anger to retribution, Norman urges them to control their rage.

The Lesson

Don't let anyone else control your emotions.

In November 2024 I broke up with the news. I cut off my access to news websites, unfollowed news outlets on my social media feeds, and taught my YouTube algorithm not to share news with me. The reason I did this is that I was obsessed with political news. I was constantly refreshing every minute, constantly looking at what happened, how people responded, and how other people responded to that response.

I realized that my emotions and my mood were being affected by people I had never met or knew anything about. My emotional state each day was being dictated by forces way outside of my control. The same was true of coworkers, friends, and family. I gave people power over me that allowed them to dictate my mood. The worst part is that they didn't even know it. They didn't give any thought to me and how I was feeling. It was like they were controlling a bull-dozer that they weren't even aware existed.

It has taken a lot of work to take that power back and to own my emotions. As Norman was trying to impart to the Bloods, we should control and use our emotions as we see fit. Their anger, while justified, would be better aimed at solving the problem, not causing more problems. Killing a bunch of people who have the same skin tone as the people who killed your icon would not solve the problem or punish those responsible for the systemic discrimination of an entire race. Use that anger, but only when it's of your choice and purpose.

I'm not saying stick your head in the sand and ignore the world. But there's a thin line between informed and obsessed.

I have channeled my depression, anxiety, and anger into all types of collaborative and artistic endeavors, including the writing of this book. Rather than lash out in unproductive ways or engage in destructive behavior, I choose to create things that help others through their darkest moments.

Deadpool & Wolverine (2024)

Starring Ryan Reynolds, Hugh Jackman

The Quote

WOLVERINE: *You couldn't even save a relationship with a goddamn stripper! And motherfucker, I wish I could say you'd die alone, but it's one of God's best jokes that you can't die, except that's on ALL OF US!*

The Context

Deadpool has pulled an unwilling Wolverine into a journey through an alternate universe in the hopes of saving his friends and their entire prime universe. Along the way, they find every way to not see eye to eye. Finally, in a moment of anger, Wolverine unleashes a tirade that points out all of Deadpool's flaws. Deadpool, the person who always has a biting comeback, is uncharacteristically silent.

The Lesson

For friends to truly help each other evolve, honesty is essential.

Daredevil (2015-2018)

Season 3, Episode 13: A New Napkin

Starring Charlie Cox, Deborah Ann Woll, Elden Henson

The Quote

MATT MURDOCK: *You don't get to destroy who I am. You will go back to prison, and you will live the rest of your miserable life in a cage knowing you'll never have Vanessa, that this city rejected you. IT BEAT YOU! I BEAT YOU!*

The Context

Vigilante Matt Murdock and crime boss Wilson Fisk have been at war for years, fighting for the soul of Hell's Kitchen. In the final showdown, Fisk goads Murdock into killing him instead of returning to prison. Although Matt has every reason to kill him, he chooses not to because that is not who he is. He feels satisfied knowing that he defeated Fisk and that Fisk will live with the knowledge that he has been truly beaten.

The Lesson

Don't let anyone define who you are.

My father had a plan and a vision for how I would live my life. He had it before I was born and still believed his path for me was the right one until he died. When I decided to follow my own path, he berated me incessantly. For a long time, I regretted disappointing him. Eventually, I realized that his disappointment was his own and had nothing to do with me. I had to make the right choices for myself and ignore his feelings. In the end, I believe he, in his own way, begrudgingly accepted my path.

By taking my life into my own hands, I no longer allowed him to destroy who I was. How dramatic would it have been if I could have stood face-to-face with him and said, "I BEAT YOU!"? But that would have been cruel and not nearly as satisfying as it was for Matt. Every moment and choice I make is a way for me to confront the negative feelings of the past and say "I BEAT YOU!", putting them back in the miserable cage they belong in, and moving forward as the whole person I am.

My father was not a villain. He was a flawed human who just wanted the best for me. The feelings of inadequacy and self-destruction are the real villains to overcome. Stay vigilant in protecting your soul.

Doctor Strange (2016)

Starring Benedict Cumberbatch, Chiwetel Ejiofor, Rachel McAdams, Tilda Swinton

The Quote

THE ANCIENT ONE: *You cannot beat a river into submission; you have to surrender to its curren, and use its power as your own. Surrender. Silence your ego, and your power will rise.*

The Context

Dr. Stephen Strange is struggling to master the mystic arts. He has an analytical mind and is trying to grasp something rooted in faith. His new mentor, the Ancient One, encourages him to surrender to the current of power he is eager to understand.

The Lesson

Surrender to the flow of life.

This quote has been my guiding principle since I saw the movie. We spend our lives desperately trying to control our surroundings. From our children and family members to entire countries, we try to shape the world around us. Whether for a sense of safety and belonging or out of pure boredom, we attempt to control the outcome of our lives. The problem is that our lives are not ours to control. There are more elements in our existence that we don't have control over than ones we do.

We set goals and steer our sails toward them, no matter what. We measure each moment by how close or how far we are from that goal. If we reach it, we set another destination. If we don't, we beat ourselves up emotionally. We strive to be the captains of our ships, but the current takes us wherever it wants.

Life happens. We have no idea what will occur in the next second, yet we make five- and ten-year plans and fixate on them incessantly. Meanwhile, there are forces at work that shape our future without any input from us. Every person we meet, every decision made by someone we've never met, can change our trajectory in unimaginable ways.

This was never more evident than in the spring of 2020. With the spread of germs that most of us will never see, every single life on Earth was changed forever. Plans were affected. Vacations were canceled. Loved ones died alone. Some relationships ended. Others began. Bonds were strengthened or weakened. Goals were abandoned. New life missions were formed. We did things we never thought we would do. And a whole generation learned how to make sourdough bread. All of this was triggered by something completely out of our control. To make matters worse, world governments reacted in ways we also had no control over. All we could do was surrender to the events and make whatever choices we could at each moment.

This quote helped me see how little control I have and that by surrendering to the current of my life, I can truly live the life I am meant to live. As much as I want to win an award for my work, all I can do is finish the project to the best of my ability. Whether it is even shared or awarded will be up to history. I've applied for hundreds of jobs in my life. All I could do was put my best foot forward in each application. Maybe there was someone I knew inside the company I could reach out to. In the end, many others had to make decisions that determined whether I got the role I was meant for. The ripple effect goes further. Someone had to hire the people who considered whether they would hire me. I had no control over those circumstances.

Ego, however, would disagree. The ego thinks it is able to will anything and everything into existence–the right job, relationship, house, family, and friends are all out there for the taking. Bosses try to control their employees. Sexual abusers try to control their victims under the guise of entitlement. We even try to control our children's lives by dictating what they should do. Those desperate to become parents stop at nothing to make it happen, regardless of the damage it can cause their bodies.

Desiring things in life is only human. Trying to control the outcome can be potentially destructive. It's better to be aware of what forces are in control of each moment and allow whatever happens to happen. Surrender. Be thankful for what you have and for what the forces of life provide, and "your power will rise."

The Fate of the Furious (2017)

Starring Vin Diesel, Dwayne Johnson, Charlize Theron

The Quote

HOBBS: *I will beat you like a Cherokee drum.*

The Context

Hobbs (played by "the Rock") and Shaw don't get along well. Now they are locked in neighboring cells in prison. As they keep provoking each other (building up to their upcoming buddy spy movie), Hobbs shouts, "I will beat you like a Cherokee drum!"

The Lesson

Don't mess with the Rock.

Godzilla (2014)

Starring Aaron Taylor-Johnson, Elizabeth Olsen, Bryan Cranston, Ken Watanabe

The Quote

DR. ISHIRO SERIZAWA: *The arrogance of man is thinking nature is in our control and not the other way around. Let them fight.*

The Context

Godzilla and two massive monsters called MUTOs are wreaking havoc across the globe. They're heading straight for San Francisco. Every attempt by humans to destroy or stop them has failed. Dr. Serizawa, who's been studying these creatures for years, finally recognizes they're a natural force. Perhaps the only way for humanity to survive is to get out of the way of Godzilla's battle with the MUTOs.

The Lesson

Stop trying to control everything and let go.

Humanity has a tremendously large ego. We try to control everything, from the forces of nature to the people we see on the street. History is filled with failed attempts to control the uncontrollable and the disastrous fallout that ensues.

As a producer and a parent I've had my ego knocked down to Earth. I have realized that I do not have control over anything. Some would say we have control only over ourselves, but even that is a lie. We have some control over our actions in the present moment. But how many times have you experienced an emotion you didn't want–a crippling sadness or depression you didn't choose? No matter what you do or want, you're going to feel that emotion for as long as it lasts.

We cannot control the people in our lives, the actions of our governments, the forces of nature, or our own emotions. And that causes stress and fear. Our own arrogance in thinking we can control everything is what keeps us from accepting what is. We do not control these forces. We react to the forces around us. And we need to be at peace with that fact of our lives. Let the world do what it does. React accordingly.

Gotham (2014-2019)

Season 1, Episode 7: Penguin's Umbrella
Season 4, Episode 1: Pax Penguina
Season 4, Episode 11: A Dark Knight: Queen Takes Knight

Starring Ben McKenzie, Donal Logue, Robin Lord Taylor, Zabryna Guerara

The Quotes

SARAH ESSEN: *Are you insane?*

JAMES GORDON: *No. Maybe a little. Feels good.*

JAMES GORDON: *I am not giving the city over to the Penguin.*

JAMES GORDON: *From the first day I put on the badge, I was told things could never change. Gotham was corrupt. GCPD was corrupt. Criminals and low-lifes ran things. You just showed me different. Penguin will be coming. It's time we showed Gotham who we are. Suit up!*

The Context

Gotham tells the story of James Gordon's entry into and rise within the Gotham City Police Department. At first, the department and city government are completely corrupt, answering more to mob bosses than to the people they are sworn to protect.

Gordon is the embodiment of a Boy Scout as he challenges the mob and his own superiors to do what is right. When a bounty is placed on his head, his own captain asks if he's insane, to which he replies, "No. Maybe a little. Feels good." He begins to embrace the chaos but remains undeterred in his fight for justice. He stands alone as his entire precinct abandons him to the hands of assassins.

As his story unfolds, he continually refuses to give in to corruption, even as new crime boss, the Penguin, asserts his power over the city. James shouts, "I am not giving the city over to the Penguin." Later, after a deadly ambush, Gordon risks everything to save his fellow officers and the public. His allies finally turn against the Penguin and the mob, choosing to fight alongside now Captain Gordon for the city's sake. He delivers a speech inspiring the force to pursue the very corruption they once allowed to control them.

The Lesson

Resilience is the key to victory.

I always admired Gordon's resiliency in the face of overwhelming odds and countless villains. He isn't wealthy or technologically equipped like Batman. He doesn't have superpowers like Superman. He rarely wears a bulletproof vest or carries anything besides a handgun, a badge, and two fists capable of causing damage. Yet he always figures out the puzzle, charges in to save lives, and locks up the bad guys.

Sometimes he makes mistakes, trusts the wrong people, or ends up captured in an elaborate scheme designed to kill him slowly. But no matter the situation, he will always fight for the soul of Gotham and believe that good people are worth saving. Whether they shun him or just stand by passively, his fellow officers are constantly watching his heroic moves.

Gordon's journey is a straightforward line of consistent goodness. It's inspiring to see the people around him shift from aiding the villains to quietly staying neutral, and then ultimately taking pride in the badge, the uniform, and everything they represent.

His resilience serves as the example they needed to do the right thing. It's his resilience that saved the city from destroying itself.

The Hangover Part II (2011)

Starring Bradley Cooper, Ed Helms, Zach Galifianakis, Ken Jeong

The Quote

MR. CHOW: *Principle? Nigga, please! We both dead inside.*

The Context

Crazy international criminal Mr. Chow—a key antagonist and source of chaos for this film's main characters—is in trouble. A former associate has just reported him to the authorities. When the rat reveals himself, he tells Chow that even though Chow keeps stealing more and more money from him, it's the principle. Chow immediately fires back, "Principle? Nigga, please! We both dead inside."

The Lesson

Always have an excellent retort ready to fire back at a moment's notice.

Seriously. That is the only lesson here. I just thought the quote was one of the most hilarious responses I ever heard.

Harry Potter and the Deathly Hallows: Part 2 (2011)

Starring Daniel Radcliffe, Emma Watson, Rupert Grint, Sir Michael Gambon

The Quote

HARRY POTTER: *Is this all real? Or is it just happening inside my head?*

PROFESSOR ALBUS DUMBLEDORE: *Of course it's happening inside your head, Harry. Why should that mean that it's not real?*

The Context

Evil Lord Voldemort has just vanquished Harry Potter. Rather than die, Harry goes to an in-between space with his recently departed headmaster, Dumbledore. They talk about what has taken place and the fact that Harry has a choice to return to the living or simply pass on. Harry questions whether all of this is real or a part of his imagination. Dumbledore replies, "Of course it's happening inside your head, Harry. Why should that mean that it's not real?"

The Lesson

It doesn't matter whether our world is real or simulated; if it is real to us, that's what matters.

I don't know whether all of this is actually happening or not. My fingers typing on this Bluetooth keyboard (while my friends talk over their second rounds of beer) could be real, or I could be imagining the sounds I hear and the touch and pressure of the keys. Life could truly be a dream. If it is real, then so be it. If it's a dream, my mind makes it feel real. Either way, if my mind believes it, then it's true.

I use this quote to remind myself not to get caught up in the philosophical debate about realism. The debate itself is an important part of human experience and should not be limited. But I act knowing that everything I am experiencing should be honored and accepted as a real part of my journey.

When I was a kid growing up as an only child, I imagined or thought for years that there was a team of people living inside my body. They would communicate with each other and with me regularly. There was one in my head, one in my heart, two on my shoulders, and two in my hips. They would work to keep my body going; if I had shoulder pain, that person would fix the issue. Same for my knee. The hip worker would do everything to keep that body part functioning.

Each had a name, their own personality, and they would work to keep me going. They would talk to each other and to me as I dealt with the day's events and my dad's arguments. They kept me company.

As an adult, I fully realize that this concept is not possible or realistic. But I accept that at that moment, it felt real, and it helped me feel less alone. Whether or not it was real is irrelevant. I felt it was real, I learned from it, and I didn't get so lost in it that I avoided being rational. Our heads and brains are real, so the thoughts flowing through them should be real too.

Harry accepted the lessons he learned from this "hallucination" and found the strength to come back to life and face his true enemy. We should learn to work with the thoughts that flow through our minds, whether they seem real or not. Our minds are the one friend we are connected to every moment of our lives. Accept the reality your mind has created.

The Imitation Game (2014)

Starring Benedict Cumberbatch, Keira Knightley, Matthew Goode

The Quote

JOAN CLARKE: *I think that sometimes it is the people who no one imagines anything of, who do the things no one … can imagine.*

The Context

Alan Turing is a brilliant cryptographer with almost no social skills. He builds a machine that allows the Allies to decipher encrypted German messages, helping win World War II. He has faced bullying, marginalization, and discrimination throughout his life. At his lowest point, his longtime partner Joan reminds him that "it is the people who no one imagines anything of, who do the things no one … can imagine."

The Lesson

Great things can come from the least expected places.

I love food. I love discovering new and interesting restaurants as well as trusty favorites. I am also a bit of a gullible person. It is hard for me to know whether someone is joking or serious.

In 2016 I started working for a nonprofit named Digital Promise. The offices were in a warehouse/startup campus area south of San Francisco with few food options. On my first day, my bosses said we would go to lunch. I said, "Of course! I like lunch." Then they said we were going to the "gas station taco place!" with an extreme amount of enthusiasm. I was skeptical. I have eaten in strange places, but never in a gas station. My first vision was spinning gross hot dogs at stations along the highway. So I was skeptical. I assumed it was a prank, but I cautiously went along with the suggestion.

Then the VP of the company, who was a respected leader in his field, said he would come along. I was still skeptical. Was he in on the joke? There was no way they could be this excited about a taco place in a nasty gas station. I reluctantly agreed to go. As we walked, we talked about work and my new coworkers and our mission, and everyone continued on their merry march to the gas station.

We passed a normal-looking Mexican restaurant with a patio, with me strangely in the front of the group. I instinctively turned into it, thinking the surprise gag would be revealed. They called out to me, "No, that's not the good one."

How good could a gas station be over a nice sit-down restaurant? I continued on, still skeptical. When we arrived, it was a typical yet cleanish gas station. The building was half convenience store, half Mexican kitchen with only a walk-up window. Like the movie *Snakes on a Plane* literally having snakes on the plane, it was literally a gas station taco joint.

Somehow, I ended up in the front of the group and had the awkward task of ordering. I was still skeptical, so I ordered two small tacos. To my surprise, my new coworkers ordered loads of burritos, tacos, tostadas, and a taco salad. Maybe my skepticism was misplaced. They obviously liked the food. That, or it was a very expensive and elaborate first-day prank. Since there was no place to sit, we walked back to the office and sat down to eat.

To my utter shock, the tacos were the best, most flavorful food I had ever had. My joy at being proven wrong about the quality of the food was replaced by regret that I bought so little of it. When I finished my two small tacos, I realized everyone else was barely halfway through their respective meals.

In that moment, I realized that even though I had no reason to look down on the suggestion that desirable food could come from a gas station, I still did. If a place like that could take the time and care to create authentic and delicious food, any place could do the same–as long as it has the ingredients to do so.

The same could be said of people. We look at an individual and immediately form an uninformed opinion of what to expect from them. We think they're capable only of the little we see superficially. We make judgments and decisions and often stick to them when we should be more curious about the person.

It's natural for humans to have biases, but we should also accept them for what they are: uninformed opinions. Great things can come from the most unlikely places, like gas stations. Allow yourself to be surprised.

Interstellar (2014)

Starring Matthew McConaughey, Anne Hathaway, Jessica Chastain, Josh Stewart

The Quote

CASE: *It's not possible.*
COOPER: *No. It's necessary.*

The Context

Earth is facing a global crop blight and a resulting dust bowl that will render the planet uninhabitable. Former NASA pilot Cooper and his crew aboard multiple spacecraft venture to another galaxy to save humanity. Their larger spaceship experiences an explosion, is spinning out of control, and is about to enter a nearby planet's atmosphere, which will lead to certain destruction.

Cooper makes a quick decision to chase the larger spaceship in their much smaller vehicle. His onboard android tells him it's impossible to catch up with, match the spin of, and successfully save the ship and the mission. Cooper responds that, while it is impossible, it is still necessary.

The Lesson

Resilience is everything.

If I had a dollar for every time someone told me something was impossible, only for me to prove otherwise, I would be very rich. My joy comes from understanding what needs to be done and showing that it can be done. This doesn't stem from ego or a need to prove my worth; it arises from the necessity of the moment.

A producer is limited by time, budget, and human needs, which can influence a project's outcome. There are many levers to pull to succeed, and it requires knowing every aspect of the creative process, logistics, and people involved to make the necessary adjustments.

The same principles apply when packing a suitcase or preparing a car for a road trip. You have no choice but to pack everything in a manner that will fit the space available. I am quite skilled at Tetris and bring that same skill to packing. There's always a way, and the final answer isn't clear until the car is fully packed.

The key is to take it one step at a time while keeping the final goal in mind. When a problem arises that threatens to prevent us from completing our day, some people will complain endlessly, wasting valuable time. Others might try to solve every problem at once, which can cause more stress or lead to solutions clashing, creating new issues.

It's helpful to consider what is the one thing you can do right now to move toward a positive result? Then ask, How did that affect the situation? What's the next thing you can do? Watch the results unfold. Repeat this process until you look up and realize the day has passed, and what you have is what you were meant to achieve.

Cooper did everything he could, then relied on his human and android crew to each play a role in taking the next steps to catch and rescue the ship and continue their mission.

It's easy to point out what's not possible before it's been proven impossible or possible. The hard part is staying resilient and boldly marching toward the necessary solution. Not every outcome, project, or mission is essential. But when it is, focus on taking every step you can with the time available, and let the future reveal whether it was possible or not.

Kung Fu Panda 2 (2011)

Starring (voices) Jack Black, Angelina Jolie, Dustin Hoffman, Michelle Yeoh

The Quote

SOOTHSAYER: *Your story may not have such a happy beginning, but that doesn't make you who you are. It is the rest of your story, who you choose to be. So, who are you, panda?*

The Context

Po is a panda who was orphaned, raised by a goose, and has learned Kung Fu. Oh, and he's the Dragon Warrior. He is on a journey to find inner peace, but he struggles with understanding his identity.

While fighting his current opponent, Shen, he sees flashes of his birth parents but has trouble recalling the full memory. Distracted, Shen gains the upper hand and hits Po so hard that Po is launched far away to a town in the distance. He loses consciousness while floating in a creek.

When he regains consciousness, a soothsayer helps him unlock the memory of his parents, revealing that they were chased and killed by Shen and his minions. This saddens him. But the soothsayer reminds him that it is not only the beginning that shapes who we are. He then sees all the good things that define him: his adoptive father, his team, his mentor, and his own journey to becoming the Dragon Warrior.

The Lesson

We are not defined by just one thing, but by everything.

Our lives are made of all types of moments:

- good
- bad
- exciting
- boring
- memorable
- forgettable
- busy
- calm
- stressful
- emotional
- boring (yes, I put it twice, because movies tend to edit out the many boring parts of the characters, and our lives)

We tend to define our identity by simple parameters:

- where we grew up
- where we go to school
- where we live
- our career
- our volunteering
- our hobby
- our relationship or marital status
- our dietary or allergy status
- our lives as parents

The sum of our lives is more than what we can add to a dating app profile. Every single moment of our lives has led us to this point, including where we are physically right now, reading these words, and these words, and these words. This is the result of billions of moments and choices that add up to the present.

We also tend to focus on the negative aspects of the past to define our identity. Trauma is a powerful force. I was emotionally abused by my father for the nineteen years I lived with him. Every mistake I made resulted in hours or days of berating, having things taken away, and being denied social experiences that most children need to build a healthy adulthood.

On one hand, I could highlight that part of my life on every social profile and CV I have. Some people need to use that pain to become who they are and create a life, ensuring others escape their pain. On the other hand, I can ignore it and pretend it never happened. Some people do this as a coping mechanism. Others are in denial and never learn from that pain.

I chose to acknowledge my pain and all the many moments in between. No one part of my story defines me. It all matters. The boat trip I couldn't take when I was fifteen because I didn't retile the bathtub perfectly taught me how to admit I was not capable of every task. The many moments I was home alone, watching movies and listening to soundtracks repeatedly. The friends I made at eighteen helping me build a life after I ran away on my nineteenth birthday. The woman who was the dad I needed in my twenties. The bad dates and the deep kisses. The moment my wife chose me, and when my son first held my hand.

All of it matters. All of it is who I am. All of it propels me forward. The same is true for you. Embrace every moment of your journey.

Mission: Impossible – Fallout (2018)

Starring Tom Cruise, Henry Cavill, Ving Rhames

The Quote

ETHAN HUNT: *I'll figure it out.*

The Context

Impossible Missions Force Field Agent Ethan Hunt is on a dangerous mission with many twists and turns. With each twist, the next steps seem impossible. When problems and oddities are pointed out to him, he has the same response: "I'll figure it out."

The Lesson

Perserverence and trust are essential.

When faced with a terrible situation, Hunt believes that he and his team will prevail. Why? Because they have to. The fate of countless lives depends on it. How does he do it?

- First, he starts with a clear objective: "What is our ultimate goal?"
- Then, he develops an overall plan for how the mission can unfold, considering multiple contingencies.
- Next, he gathers a team he can trust and the tools that can support them along the way.
- Then, he acts on his plan.
- When something goes wrong (and this is key to the point), he stays focused on the next step he can take to keep the plan moving forward.

He knows that the path to a successful mission is not a straight, solid line but more of a squiggly dotted path with a few obstacles thrown in to keep it interesting. The same can be said of the making of the *Mission Impossible* movies themselves.

The filmmakers behind this series treat each movie as an impossible mission they must complete. They have a clear goal in mind, but with each situation, they "figure it out" and make the necessary choices to succeed in the moment. With preparation for multiple possible outcomes, they take a winding journey to reach a finished movie or deliver an experience for audiences to enjoy (or criticize).

Life is made up of billions of moments when a step must be taken or a decision need to be made. The past is gone, and the future is not yet here. All you can do is trust that when each moment and challenge appears, you will figure it out. Whether Ethan believes he will find a solution or is lying to his team, he inspires trust in those around him by showing that he, and they, can figure it out. And his perserverance resilience is truly inspiring.

The Quote

ETHAN HUNT: *We'll burn that bridge when we get to it.*

The Context

Ethan is moments away from coming face-to-face with his ruthless enemy. When asked what he will do when the moment comes, Ethan replies, "We'll burn that bridge when we get to it."

The Lesson

One thing at a time.

This is one of my favorite quotes. I have been in too many situations where the people I am sharing space with are trying to figure out everything that can or will happen. I don't subscribe to that thinking because you can spend so much time trying to plan the future that you miss living in the present. And nothing ever goes exactly to plan.

I love that this quote is a combination of "crossing the bridge when we get to it" and "burning bridges." As a producer, you have to solve one problem at a time. When you add up all the solutions, you get a complete project. In the meantime, deal with what you can in that moment and leave the rest for future you to handle.

So-and-so is going to be upset when they find out about that. Can we do anything about it right now? Yes? Let's fix it. No? Then we'll burn that bridge when we get to it.

That artwork didn't turn out the way we planned. Can we fix it right now? Yes? Let's go! No? It's the weekend and they're closed? Then we'll burn that bridge when we get to it.

Think of it as a fun way to delay dealing with problems until you're able to handle them.

The Quote

AUGUST WALKER: *Why do you have to make this so fucking complicated?*

The Context

In the interest of avoiding spoilers, this mission context is classified.

The Lesson

Simply put, I know many people who make things much more complicated than necessary. They try to fix every problem immediately, no matter how impossible, stressful, or destructive it may be. They add more steps than truly needed to solve the issue. And some complain about every problem they face instead of talking about solutions or accepting they have no control over the problem and focusing on what they can do (I'm looking at you, Brits, complaining about the weather every ten minutes).

I am a great simplifier. What is the wider problem? What is the real reason behind it? What is the one thing we can do right now to fix it? Let's do it and see where it takes us. That's why I admire characters like Ethan Hunt, Jack Bauer, Captain Picard, and President Bartlett. They are aware of the complexities of the big picture but are able to focus their teams on the problem at hand. There are times in which complexity is warranted, but not every situation or solution is complicated.

To those people who make every problem into an insurmountable complex nightmare, I say to myself (and a few times out loud), "Why do you have to make this so fucking complicated?" First it makes me chuckle, and laughter is truly the best medicine. Then it helps me take a step back and ask myself, Am I simplifying because I'm impatient in this moment, or is this problem actually a fucking complicated issue? Even though I am a simplifier, above all, I am flexible.

Miss Sloane (2016)

Starring Jessica Chastain, Mark Strong, Gugu Mbatha-Raw

The Quote

ELIZABETH SLOANE: *Lobbying is about foresight. About anticipating your opponent's moves and devising countermeasures. The winner plots one step ahead of the opposition. And plays her trump card just after they play theirs. It's about making sure you surprise them. And they don't surprise you.*

The Context

Miss Sloane follows Elizabeth Sloane, a brilliant and ruthless Washington D.C. lobbyist who defies expectations when she refuses to support a powerful pro-gun initiative and instead joins a smaller firm fighting for stricter gun control. As she orchestrates an aggressive, ethically fraught campaign, Sloane pushes her team—and herself—to the breaking point while becoming the target of political retaliation. Her relentless pursuit of victory culminates in a high-stakes congressional showdown that forces her to face the personal and professional consequences of her uncompromising tactics.

The Lesson

Everything is like a chess game.

I owe a lot to chess. When I was in elementary school, I joined the chess club. I had no dreams of excelling at it, but it helped me in many ways outside of the game.

As a player, I learned to see the entire board, not just the next move I wanted to make. As a producer, I learned to see the whole set, schedule, and situation, not just what I needed to happen.

As a player, I understood that each piece moves differently and has unique strategic advantages and disadvantages. As a producer, I realized that everyone is different, living and moving in their own ways. They have specific motivations and unique ways of giving and receiving praise and criticism.

As a player, I learned how to read my opponent to gauge how cautious or impulsive they are. Do they charge in blindly or carefully consider every move before touching a piece? As a producer, the same applies. I need to read the person across the meeting table or video call to determine how serious they are about the project, whether they will follow through on their commitments or they might flake and not deliver.

As a player, I understood how to look ahead and map out possible outcomes, including where danger could come from. As a producer, I look at the next steps and how any of them could threaten the project or the people involved before I send that critical email.

Lastly, as a player I learned how to win gracefully, lose with acceptance, and learn from my mistakes. As a producer, I understand that not every situation can be won; sometimes I must accept a less-than-ideal outcome and move on to the next project.

Elizabeth was an expert at reading her opponents and making the right moves at the right times. She even had to sacrifice many pieces along the way, but her resilience allowed her to keep her queen hidden in plain sight long enough so that when she struck, she put her opponent away in one swift move.

In short, strategy games can be very helpful in understanding real-world situations. You have to be open to different types of people and be flexible in any situation that arises. You can't control everything that might happen—only the moves you make. Be adaptable to whatever reactions your actions provoke, and always think ahead.

Molly's Game (2017)

Starring Jessica Chastain, Idris Elba, Kevin Costner

The Quote

LARRY BLOOM: *I'm your father. Trying to comprehend how much I love you would be like trying to visualize the size of the universe.*

The Context

Molly Bloom has spent her life resenting her father for reasons she's not entirely sure of. She also faces trial for allegedly running an illegal poker operation. Despite these issues, her father appears in her moment of need to help her understand why she has acted the way she has and how it connects to her feelings about him.

He tells her that he still loves her, and he does so with an eloquence that all parents might wish they could emulate.

The Lesson

A parent's love is forever.

Until you become a parent, it's hard to truly understand what love really is. In relationships and marriage, love can be based on intimacy, sexual attraction, or infatuation. While those fleeting feelings can turn into love, you are still not fully responsible for that person's life, and breakups can happen at any time.

The same applies to loving a parent or family member. In the early years, that love is rooted in dependency–you have to love the people caring for and with you every day, through all your developmental stages.

But when you hold a child in your arms for the first time, you truly understand what love is. This little person will depend on you forever. You'll always need to be aware of their whereabouts, actions, and thoughts. And you must accept them for who they are, which means you need to learn about them. You study everything from their emotional reactions to, at least in early years, every bowel movement.

Unlike in movies, you must be present for every moment, not just the dramatic ones. In real life, you embrace every mundane, boredom-filled moment and find ways to help them engage and discover themselves, all while keeping your ego in check. You have to help them become the best they can be, despite your own wishes for their lives.

That is where my father fell short. He loved me, but he loved the version of me he wanted to see. He never took the opportunity to truly learn who I am. That's unfortunate because I was still discovering myself while fighting the inner voice that was being shaped for me. No parent is perfect. It's easy to look back on his life and point out his failings. But he put in the effort to keep me alive and teach me the lessons I needed to get here today. He loved me.

That kind of love is beyond measure. And now, as I'm a parent myself, I see love in a totally new light. I wouldn't trade this experience for anything in the world. I love you, Skylar.

Rogue One: A Star Wars Story (2016)

Starring Felicity Jones, Diego Luna, Ben Mendelsohn, Donnie Yen, Jiang Wen

The Quote

CHIRRUT ÎMWE: *I'm one with the Force, and the Force is with me.*

The Context

Chirrut is a guardian of the Jedi temple on Jedha. He is blind, yet skilled. Although he isn't a Jedi, he is sensitive to and a believer in the Force.

The Lesson

Believe.

Even though the Force is an idea created for the Star Wars universe, I do believe there is a serendipitous force that exists in our world. Many believe in God, a god, or several gods. Others believe that nothing but science drives our existence. I believe in two things: First, everyone is entitled to believe in what they believe and that which brings them comfort. Second, I have seen evidence of moments coming together that I can't explain, which have worked in my favor, and I choose to believe that something exists that has not yet revealed itself or proven its existence.

I have experienced many moments that came together with split-second timing and literally put a smile on my face. Some would call that luck, others would call it God's interference, and some would ignore the moment altogether.

I believe it is important to honor those moments. I also do not feel the need to define the force that might have caused them. My soul is at peace, trusting that all will take place as it was meant to. Not that it is predesigned, but when the moment passes, we know that is how it was supposed to happen. I believe that everything is how it was meant to be.

And I don't need you to believe what I believe. Religion can be helpful in fostering a sense of community and hope. But the flaw in religion is that people think it's a gauge of how right they are, and that everyone who believes differently is wrong. Belief doesn't need an audience. Chirrut did not need everyone to believe what he believed. He trusted in the Force, and the Force was with him. That's all anyone needs–to believe what they believe.

The Quote

BAZE MALBUS: *Good luck!*

CHIRRUT ÎMWE: *I don't need luck! I have you!*

The Context

Chirrut's loyal companion, Baze, is dedicated to safeguarding him.

The Lesson

Honor the special people in your life.

Friends and family are incredibly important. I hope you have many people you can rely on in times of need and joy. While I have many close friends and a few who have made genuine sacrifices for me, there are three who I can truly call my heroes–those who saved my life without knowing the impact it would have.

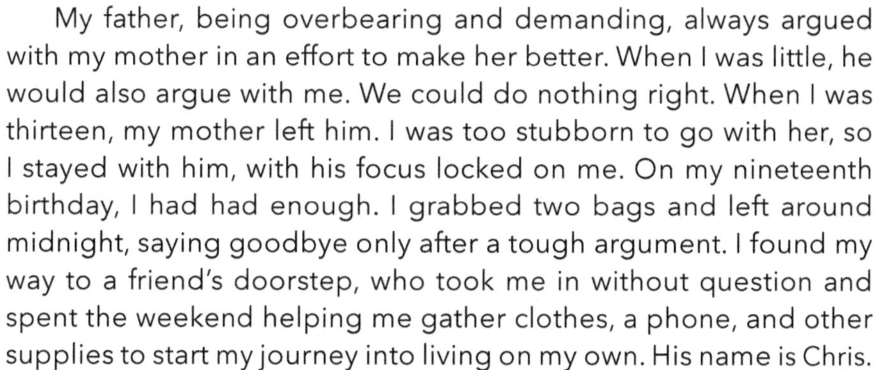

My father, being overbearing and demanding, always argued with my mother in an effort to make her better. When I was little, he would also argue with me. We could do nothing right. When I was thirteen, my mother left him. I was too stubborn to go with her, so I stayed with him, with his focus locked on me. On my nineteenth birthday, I had had enough. I grabbed two bags and left around midnight, saying goodbye only after a tough argument. I found my way to a friend's doorstep, who took me in without question and spent the weekend helping me gather clothes, a phone, and other supplies to start my journey into living on my own. His name is Chris.

Not long after, I completed a freelance job for a department at the college I attended. I was supposed to get paid before Christmas, but red tape caused the delay until well after New Year's. I had no money to get through the holidays. Out of the kindness of her heart, my boss, Kari, gave me $1,000 to help me survive.

Recently, I worked for a company that was making layoffs across the board. My role was being cut. I didn't know where I would work next, but I believed I would end up where I was meant to be. During that long process, someone I had mentored years earlier had an opening at his new company. He recommended me, and after several interviews I landed my dream job the same day my current role was being eliminated. The timing was perfect. His name is Deep.

Like everyone on Earth, I have experienced many challenging moments. I realized that I don't need luck; I have Naomi, Skylar, Mema, Betty, Sara, Kari, Deep, Chris, Pat, Spence, Aly, Heather, Lindsey, Raquel, Dave, Aylara, Selina, Ingrid, Neysa, Amy, Shannon, Hopper, Keith, Angela, Kristin, Dale, Amber, Ronn, Charlie, Bruis, Kevin, Joan, Kat, Juan, Mario, Alex, Andrew, JVD, Kevin, Chelsea, Jo, Cooksey, Paul, James, Leah, Becky, Alex, Andy, Natasha, Alex, Gabriel, Todor, Elisa, Mathis, Ami, and so many more.

The right people will come to help you at the right moment in your life. All you can do is be thankful and take the next step forward.

The Quote

CASSIAN ANDOR: *Make ten men feel like a hundred.*

The Context

A small group of rebels secretly infiltrates an Imperial stronghold. Their mission is to find the plans for the Death Star and transmit them to the rest of the rebellion. Outnumbered massively, Jyn and Cassian lay out the plan. Jyn says, "If we can make it to the ground, we'll take the next chance. And the next. On and on until we win ... or the chances are spent." Cassian adds that they can use their limited numbers and resources to spread out and cause enough chaos and confusion to "make ten men feel like one hundred" and distract the enemy from their true goal.

The Lesson

One person is capable. A team is powerful!

From African dance festivals to student films and from documentaries to productions with COVID protocols, I have led teams to the successful completion of hundreds of projects. Maybe even a thousand. More often than not, it wasn't the technology, the newest camera, or computer software that got us through the many tough days and nights.

It was the people who made magic happen. Those who were knowledgeable and eager for a challenge. Those who were inexperienced yet hungry for the experience that could turn the tide of their careers. They were ready to plan, strong enough to execute, and flexible enough to adjust when the unexpected happened. As long as I took care of them, they would always take care of the project.

If you inspire your team, inform them, and care for them, ten people can truly accomplish the impossible. They can be more focused and determined than a larger group ever could, because every one of those ten will be able to shine and claim a piece of the victory.

Sherlock Holmes: A Game of Shadows (2011)

Starring Robert Downey Jr., Jude Law, Noomi Rapace

The Quote

MADAM SIMZA HERON: *What do you see?*

SHERLOCK HOLMES: *Everything. That is my curse.*

The Context

Sherlock is dancing with his client, Simza, in the middle of a fancy party. She surveys the crowd, looking for signs of who the killer might be before they strike the currently unknown victim. She asks Sherlock what he sees, and he replies that his curse is that he sees everything.

The Lesson

If I could have any superpower, it would be the ability to see and hear everything happening in the room. At a party, I can focus on my conversation while simultaneously knowing who is talking to whom, what topics they are discussing, and recalling where everyone was at each stage of the night. It's a sense I can't turn off. I am hyper-aware of my surroundings.

As a producer, this sense serves me well. As the day goes on, I am constantly aware of what everyone is doing, what conversations they're having, what calls they hear and which ones they miss, and overall what each of them knows or doesn't know. With this information, I can pull the right strings to guide the crew through the day and achieve the goals of the shoot. Sometimes I don't even have to do anything.

But there are times when people need help. Someone might be fading and in need of a caffeine boost or a kind word. The tech might be failing, and a distraction is needed to keep morale up while the technicians solve the issue. There are also times when someone isn't pulling their weight, and it helps if I can see the signs and respond before their behavior impacts the day or the team negatively.

Every social and work situation involves multiple things happening at once. Being aware of all of them helps keep everything running smoothly. For those of us who are like Sherlock, it can be hard to turn off this sense and focus on ourselves despite the chaos around us. But it's important to find your peace amid the noise.

Spider-Man: Into the Spider-Verse (2018)

Starring (voices) Shameik Moore, Jake Johnson, Hailee Steinfeld

The Quote

MILES MORALES: *When will I know I'm ready?*

PETER B. PARKER: *You won't. It's a leap of faith. That's all it is, Miles. A leap of faith.*

The Context

Miles Morales is on his way to becoming the Spider-Man of his reality. Peter B. Parker was pulled into Miles's reality via a dimensional rift. Peter has been Spider-Man for much longer and has taken on a mentoring role for Miles. As Miles is on the edge of a building, ready to throw caution to the wind and embrace his abilities, he remembers the words of his mentor and takes the leap.

The Lesson

Every new endeavor requires a leap of faith. Take it. I have taken several leaps of faith in my life:

- Leaving my father's house with two backpacks and no money
- Breaking up with a long-term girlfriend for the right reasons
- Proposing to my wife because I thought she would make a great mom
- Accepting an on-the-spot offer to coordinate advanced practicum

- Being asked to produce numerous video projects
- Moving to San Francisco
- Moving to London
- Being asked to build a studio
- Being asked to bring teams together from merging companies
- Choosing a new job over an offer to stay in the current company
- Speaking up in a key moment that would automatically place me in a project management role

In each of these moments, there was no logic I could depend on to guarantee I would be able to succeed. I had to just make the choice and have faith that I could make it. I was blessed to have people around who could help me from moment to moment. But I had to take the leap needed to accept the change in my life.

The largest leap of faith I ever could have taken was having a child. Every day with him is a leap of faith. Unlike jobs and projects, there is a large margin of error if I fail as a parent. But from the moment he was conceived, I had no choice but to take the leap and have faith that I would do everything I could to help him grow in a healthy way. Eleven years in, and the leaps have thus far been rewarded.

We all have moments like the above. It helps to acknowledge them and then take the leap.

Tenet (2020)

Starring John David Washington, Robert Pattinson, Elizabeth Debicki

The Quote

NEIL: *What's happened, happened.*

The Context

Tenet follows a CIA operative who joins a secret organization to stop a villain using a technology that can send objects and people moving backward through time. As he navigates twisting timelines and shifting alliances, he races to prevent a temporal catastrophe that could end the world.

In the end we are told by the operative's partner that events in the past cannot be changed, even by traveling or moving backward through time.

The Lesson

Embrace what is.

I used to have a sense of anxiety about the things I couldn't control. The paths not taken. The choices not made. The options that could have been better. But now it fills me with comfort to know that whatever occurred did so in the way it was intended, and it couldn't have happened a different way. Wherever I am is where I am meant to be. The problems I am facing are the trials I'm meant to learn from at that moment.

Whichever path or course of action that is considered "right" doesn't matter. Would you rather live with the anxiety of all the things you have no control over, or with the comfort that whatever takes place is the way it was intended to be and the reality that is yours to embrace? I don't see it as complacency; I see it as the sanest way to live.

Top Gun: Maverick (2022)

Starring Tom Cruise, Miles Teller, Jennifer Connelly

The Quote

BRADLEY "ROOSTER" BRADSHAW: *Come on, Mav, do some of that pilot shit!*

The Context

Mav and Rooster are escaping enemy territory in an old fighter jet. They are spotted and pursued by pilots in newer-generation jets. Mav is one of the most talented pilots in the service, but he is outmatched, outgunned, and worried about getting his copilot killed. Rooster gets Mav's head back in the game by shouting, "Come on, Mav, do some of that pilot shit!" Mav then pulls out every pilot trick he can to save their lives.

The Lesson

Even a badass needs a reminder that they are a badass.

As a producer, you have to inspire the people around you. Everyone has personal lives, interpersonal issues, and health concerns that can impact their performance on the job. It is your job to boost them and make them feel heard so they can bring their best to the mission.

While supporting other people in any type of situation, you should always be aware of where you are. How are your energy levels? Where is your motivation? What do you need to get through the day? What is blocking you from fixing the problem in front of you?

I have found this quote to be a great way to motivate me and remind myself that I am someone who has bested (or at least survived) every problem I have ever faced. I take liberties and modify The Quote to fit my own personality:

"Come on, Mav, do some of that pilot shit!"

becomes

"Come on, D, do some of that producer shit!"

It's a way of calling on my past self as well as my producing ancestors. We all face problems that, in the moment, seem insurmountable. It helps to have a reminder that other producers have faced bigger problems than this and have succeeded in getting their movies out, and that I, too, can call on that legacy to rise to this moment.

I hope that in your toughest moments, you have a physical copilot to remind you to "do some of that accountant shit!" or whatever type of shit you do so well:

- that artist shit!
- that parent shit!
- that engineering shit!
- that adulting shit!

Or whatever type of shit you do so well. If you don't have that person, then it is time to be your own copilot and remind yourself that you are a badass and that you will make it back to whatever aircraft carrier you call home.

X-Men: First Class (2011)

Starring James McAvoy, Michael Fassbender, Jennifer Lawrence, Kevin Bacon

The Quote

PROFESSOR CHARLES XAVIER: *You know, I believe that true focus lies somewhere between rage and serenity.*

The Context

In the first adventure of young Charles Xavier and Erik Lensherr, Erik struggles to enhance his powers. Charles, who is trying to train a new team of people with extraordinary abilities, notices the rage inside Erik.

Using his own mind-manipulation powers, he unlocks a peaceful memory from Erik's past. He tells Erik that "true focus lies somewhere between rage and serenity." With that, Erik can now use his powers in ways he never thought possible.

The Lesson

It takes time and effort to find the balance needed to persevere.

In Spring 1998, the high school guidance counselor I was closest to asked me to come to her office. I had no idea that this one moment would not only change my life but also set me on a path to becoming who I was meant to be. She handed me an application for a seminar called HOBY (Hugh O'Brien Youth Leadership Seminar), later renamed ILS (Illinois Leadership Seminar). It is an annual three-day seminar designed to help one high school sophomore from every school learn how to think independently instead of being told what to think.

I went in not knowing who I was or what I wanted to do. I knew I was a nerd/geek who followed the rules. But I mostly stayed in the background around the other students, though I stood out to my teachers and administrators.

During the seminar, I encountered activities and speakers that challenged me to see myself in a different light. To help participants come out of their shells and keep their energy up through the intense weekend, several loud and exciting cheers are taught and become second nature. They are silly at their core, but once you realize you're not the only one screaming like an enraged animal, you really get into the camaraderie of the moment.

Most of the groups were high-energy, but for some reason, my group was introverted. At first I stayed quiet, but soon I did little things that made me stand out. I asked the group why we weren't as loud as the others. I realized at that moment that people were going to be who they were. During the final evening's talent showcase, I went up to the stage to play a song from the 1944 film *Laura* that I learned on the piano. People cheered! I've performed in multiple music competitions, but this was the first time I performed in front of peers. Though we were strangers only thirty-six hours prior, we all felt like family, and I realized this was where I belonged.

When I finished my performance, instead of returning to sit with my low-energy groups I sat near the stage. I was drawn to how everyone working there seemed to be close friends, yet they worked well enough to keep the show running. There was one person named Hopper, who was the MC and truly inspired me. I stayed close to him, not knowing that one day we would run this organization in multiple ways and remain friends for over twenty years and counting.

For fifteen years, ILS and its monthly meetings, events, and preparation activities were my main volunteer outlet. It was where I learned about organizational change, crisis management, trust in your team, and resilience in the face of overwhelming exhaustion. This long and impactful story illustrates the lesson ILS taught me: when to step back and let things unfold and when to jump in and take control to turn the situation around. I even named the operations room the War Room—a title still in use today.

Even more importantly, I learned what happens when I bring the wrong approach to a situation. I would rush in when patience was needed, and I ended up making everyone angry. I would see a simple solution and try to push everyone toward it quickly, only to run into the brick wall of the more complicated nature of the individuals in a group. Once I learned how to find the balance between rage and serenity, action and calm, the organization trusted me to run seminars for two years.

Like Erik, I never thought I could play such a role. But it took the Charleses of the organization (Hopper, Kristin, Keith, Angela, April, Naomi, and many more) to help me find that point and be what the organization needed me to be. I was never able to move a large satellite dish like Erik, but I did have a hand in supporting the leadership and personal development of over 1,500 young people. I know in my heart that many of them were as inspired as I was in a college basement, next to a stage, watching a grown man in a Hawaiian shirt show a room full of teenagers how to be their best selves in the summer of 1998.

And in those moments when the rage builds and you feel the urge to destroy everything in your path, allow your inner Charles to prevail and remind you that balance is necessary. When Erik is faced with killing the man who caused his lifetime of pain, Charles tries everything he can to step in and urge calm. He tells him, "Erik, please. Be the better man. You have a gift … Erik, there will be no turning back!

Rage is easy. Serenity is a dream. Balance is the hardest place to live. But try your best, and you will find the place and the people you were meant to live with.

Outro

Movie quotes can be powerful ...

Black Panther (2018)

T'CHALLA: *We can still heal you...*

ERIK KILLMONGER: *Why, so you can lock me up? Nah. Just bury me in the ocean with my ancestors who jumped from ships, 'cause they knew death was better than bondage.*

Movie quotes can entertain ...

Any Given Sunday (1999)

LUTHER "SHARK" LAVAY: *Coach, calm down, you're gonna have a stroke!*

MONTEZUMA MONROE: *I don't get strokes muthafucka! I give 'em!*

And they can be inspirational. I hope this book has given you a quote to make it through the day.

Tombstone (1993)

CURLY BILL: *Well ... bye.*

Index

Emotional Guidance
In addition to including the films, characters and actors mentioned in this book, this index cites emotional themes, shown in **boldface**, so that you can fully access Lessons in the Lines.

#

A

B

C

D

I

J

K

L

M

N

O

S

T

U

V

W

X

Y

Z

www.ingramcontent.com/pod-product-compliance
Lightning Source LLC
LaVergne TN
LVHW010651110826
845149LV00014B/3029

* 9 7 9 8 9 9 8 9 7 2 0 5 8 *